W9-BTS-088

Love, Norm

DR. NORMAN D. FINTEL ON EQUALITY AND COURAGE IN A WORLD CALLING FOR CHANGE

Sue,
Thanks for helping us change the world!
One by One,
Barb

BARBARA FINTEL COLLINS
CO-FOUNDER, DINING FOR WOMEN

barbarafintelcollins.com

Library of Congress Control Number:2019905471

ISBN 978-1-7338277-4-4
Ebook ISBN 978-1-7338277-3-7

Cover and interior designed by Laura Blume, laurablume.com

This memoir reflects the recollection of a lifetime of experiences through writings and conversations with my father, Norman D. Fintel. As a daughter trying to honor my father's last wish for me to finish writing his book, I did the best I could. It is entirely possible that some details and sequences of events are not completely accurate.

Printed in the United States

2 3 4 5 6 7 8

First edition

NORM'S DEDICATION

To the nine grandchildren and
great grandchildren—the future.

CONTENTS

vii Foreword by Michael C. Maxey
ix Introduction—Why Now?

PROLOGUE

1 Nine Month Miracle Message

PART I: THE PLANTING SEASON

11 Chapter 1—Tilling the Soil
27 Chapter 2—Planting Seeds
43 Chapter 3—Windy Weather
55 Chapter 4—Watering the Soul
65 Chapter 5—Roots Take Hold
79 Chapter 6—Facing the Sun

PART II: THE GROWING SEASON

93 Chapter 7—Cultivation
105 Chapter 8—Branching Out
115 Chapter 9—Transplanting
133 Chapter 10—Cross Pollination
143 Photo Timeline
161 Chapter 11—Buds and Blossoms
179 Chapter 12—In Full Bloom

PART III: HARVEST SEASON

197 Chapter 13—A Man for All Seasons
215 Chapter 14—Bountiful Harvest
231 Chapter 15—Planting the Future
247 Chapter 16—Living Norm's Way

253 Acknowledgments
254 About the Author

FOREWORD

by Michael C. Maxey, President, Roanoke College

Norm Fintel, Roanoke College's eighth president, came to visit a month after I became the 11th president of the College in 2007. He encouraged me to care for the college in the way he and Jo had. He let me know, in his inimitable way, how his work there was the most "demanding and rewarding" assignment he had ever taken on in his distinguished career. He spoke about lives influenced during his tenure in office. His emphasis was on others.

Norm told me a poignant story of a visit he received early in his presidency from Roanoke College Trustee and Virginia Senator Leonard G. Muse, who told Norm, "You are not the presidency. You hold the office of the presidency." Simple, direct, humbling. Norm advised me to remember that advice.

Norm was paying it forward. Senator Muse helped him. He wanted to help me. He advised me to take the work seriously, but not take myself seriously. He had modeled that during his fourteen years as Roanoke College president and in subsequent years.

Stories of encouragement and advice for all of us abound in this book of Norm's writings. His gentle and powerful influence is also found in the stories and memories shared by his children.

During his presidency at Roanoke, he often presented to large, sometimes raucous, groups. He spoke softly but with powerful conviction. It was marvelous the way people leaned in to listen to him. He had a quiet charisma, but it was compelling and substantive. He made others long to be with him and to hear from him. This wonderful treasury of his thinking, his conviction and his influence is a gift of that quiet charisma.

Norm paid it forward throughout his life. His Christian faith, his family devotion, his crystal-clear leadership of people and institutions, his love of humanity and its goodness, shone throughout his life and it shines in this volume.

Many thanks for sharing, Norm. We will do our best to live up to your high standard.

INTRODUCTION

Why Now?

IF YOU WATCH FOR THEM, THERE ARE MOMENTS IN YOUR LIFE THAT CHANGE THE VERY ESSENCE OF HOW YOU LIVE. Moments when your mind is open at exactly the same time that wisdom strikes or at the rare times you're feeling no fear. These are the moments when it's possible to rewrite the story of your life. My father Norm's life was filled with these moments. In my own life, a few of these moments happened after he did what I thought was unthinkable—he asked me to finish writing this book. During the process I became forever addicted to living Norm's Way. After reading his story, and seeing how it became mine, I believe you might too.

A humble, everyday man, Norm Fintel's life was anything but ordinary. From the farm fields in Nebraska to the hallowed halls of academia as President of Roanoke College, his higher calling was living out the *Golden Rule* and serving humankind. He quietly planted seeds, encouraging everyone he met to become their best selves.

Always strong and healthy, when a doctor visit for a persistent ache in his clavicle led to a shocking stage 4 non-smoker lung cancer diagnosis, our family was shattered. This was in late 2016, at the same time Norm was deeply disturbed that our nation was becoming increasingly fractured. He didn't want to leave this world without trying to save it. When he asked me to help finish his book of life lessons, how could I refuse, even though I was thinking, "how am I ever going to get this done?" But I just started writing. He knew I would tap into my reservoir of fearlessness.

At the end of carving out the first draft, my first "moment" happened. I realized the depth of his influence throughout my life, most notably in 2003 when I co-founded and helped nurture Dining for Women—now the largest global giving circle movement dedicated to advancing gender equality and well-being for women and girls around the world. His example and encouragement over my lifetime led me to believe I could change the world. So I did—with the help of thousands of others. And if I can, anyone can.

With this powerful influence in mind, I went back to the beginning of the book, weaving in examples of how a father's moral code of living can so deeply affect a daughter, and showing that living Norm's Way actually works.

The first section of the book delivers what can only be called Norm's "Miracle Message." The remaining chapters chronicle his life story, embedding thirty-four life lessons, adages, and quotes from his timeless wisdom. End-of-chapter questions will engage you to reflect on your own life with gentle nudges to reframe how you live. In doing so, I hope that you are inspired and encouraged to live each day reaching for miraculous moments.

From the beginning, Norm, my editors, and I agreed this book is not about politics. Nor is it about one's faith, though Norm clearly was influenced heavily by his Lutheran heritage. There is no taking sides or passing judgment. At the core, this is a story about the power and responsibility of the individual and the expectations we demand from ourselves and others.

After my father died, the other great influencer in my life—my mom Jo—lived with us for sixteen months. After sixty-four years of marriage, there wasn't a day that she didn't wonder why she was still on earth and not with the love of her life. I'm convinced Jo lived to wake up every day to ask me "Is it done yet?" To hang on until she was sure her beloved husband's story was going to be shared with the world. Sure enough, my editor sent the final draft in what would be the last week of her life. I read the book to my mom, her eyes open to an unseen audience, unable to speak, but squeezing my hands in her favorite parts. Ten minutes after finishing the final word on the final page, she died, holding my hand. No doubt she went straight to tell Norm all about it.

In giving voice to my father's message, my own life irrevocably changed. There's no going back. I want more of what he had—that inner light of joy that comes from a life defined by moral courage and an unwavering commitment to serving humankind. What gives me hope in the churning world of today is his message and knowing there are thousands of people he touched, and thousands who are searching for Norm's practical ways to lead our best lives. When we do, we all carry on the legacy of my father.

Barb Fintel Collins and Norm Fintel, 1959 (left) and 2010 (right)

PROLOGUE

Nine Month Miracle Message

I THINK I'M ONE OF THE ONLY PEOPLE THAT CAN SAY IF I COULD GO BACK, I WOULDN'T CHANGE A SINGLE THING. HOW LUCKY AM I. I GOT EVERYTHING I NEEDED TO GET DONE DURING MY MIRACLE.

LAST WORDS OF MY FATHER, DR. NORMAN D. FINTEL

AT HEART, MY FATHER WAS A FARMER, AND PEOPLE WERE HIS CROP. He spent a lifetime planting and nourishing seeds of the soul. So, at the end of his life, when stormy weather threatened the bounty of his harvest, the weight of the world was suddenly heavy on his shoulders.

How many people do you know who, after receiving a stage 4 non-smoker lung cancer diagnosis, would spend their final nine months of remission trying to save the world? That's exactly what Norm Fintel did.

At the same time as his diagnosis, the world watched as unprecedented division and polarization rocked our very souls. Norm's angst from watching our leaders move away from a moral code of values that he devoted his lifetime to developing in others was so disturbing to him that he didn't want to leave the earth without first trying to save it.

So, when cutting-edge immunotherapy, a miracle, or his sheer will sparked a remission, he made a bold decision. He asked me to transform a small collection of life lessons originally intended for his grandchildren into a book you are now reading—with thirty-four life lessons and a message of hope for anyone searching for ways to help heal the wounds of the world.

> *Norm:* Being given remission was a miracle. I didn't do it. It's true that medicine might have done it, but it's still a miracle. And why me? Why not someone else? Haven't I done enough now? Is there something I'm supposed to do? Well, my thought was God isn't ready for me yet.

If it's possible to be humble to a fault, that would be my dad, which is why sharing his sapient wisdom was a bold move for him. He was a quiet, cerebral person who was most comfortable teaching values through example rather than words. So, when he decided to share his practical advice—words we all crave to hear—I took the opportunity and ran with it before he could change his mind.

In the months of his miracle remission, we began recording our conversations. Then I discovered 470 lifetime writings in a rickety, old file cabinet locked away in storage. This treasure trove of knowledge was buried within speeches, letters, and reflections, most of them never seen or read before, not even by my mother. It was there that the themes of his life emerged, and I learned of the influences that shaped a moral giant. It's my greatest privilege to now bring his words into the sunlight.

NORM'S LIFE DEFINING MOMENTS

Born in 1925, lucky with the gene pool and circumstances of birth, my father is an example of someone who lived life well. In our interviews I learned that his defining moments began early and struck often. Whether inspired by serendipity, luck, or blind faith, each moment opened a door for living with deeper purpose.

Raised on a farm in Nebraska and immersed in a strong German Lutheran heritage, Norm had parents who nurtured lifelong intellectual curiosity, deep faith, and a hard-work ethic along with a wide-open approach to life. At an unusually early age, my father became the leader of his life, then he devoted himself to helping others do the same.

Imagine yourself at ten years old, the age when Norm first recognized injustices based on the color of one's skin. Then imagine yourself at sixteen, which was when Norm committed his life to serving others. Then at twenty-one, the unimaginable happened when he won an airplane in his hometown lottery, an event that literally changed the course of his life. He would go on to courageously walk through many more unexpected doors as they opened, both embracing and leading change over his lifetime.

While he was best known for shaping the minds and hearts of our next generations as president of Roanoke College, in his miracle remission, I learned he was so much more than an educator or even a father. His calling was helping people be their best selves. And as he traveled the world, his eyes were opened to the values that bind all people together. These are the seeds of the soul, where we find common ground, and the heart of Norm's Miracle Message to us all.

SEEDS OF THE SOUL: PEACE, EQUALITY, LOVE

Norm's vision is of a world of peace, one where people take care of all people. Where equality rules. Where agape love and kindness thrive. Where those fortunate to be born with opportunities make sure those born without them find them. His vision is of a world without blinders of division. He places responsibility firmly in the hands of every individual and calls on us to build a movement of value-based leaders, demanding more from ourselves and our leaders. Where decisions are made based on love not hate. Tolerance not judgment. Openness not evasiveness. Integrity not deceit. Respect not negative criticism. Accountability not blame. Where our actions are founded in courage, not fear.

Wherever Norm went—whatever continent he visited—he learned what people everywhere have in common—a yearning for peace, equality, and love. Values that bind us ALL together, where unity prevails because we all speak the same language.

PEACE

Norm: The word *peace* means many things to many people. It means freedom of fear, freedom from war, from want, from misery and desolation. From cold and hunger, from greed and vengeance. Peace can still our hearts that are filled with the agony and fears of everyday life. Peace offers a security and inward knowledge of truth and perfection.

Peace cannot be won without effort, just as a battle is not won without a fight. For peace to prevail, we must live by the power of love, by the power of example, and by the power of prophecy, which says for all to hear that we must be dedicated to living in this world as we find it, loving and serving people as we find them—brother, sister, white, black, yellow, red, or brown. It is bigger than race. It's about equality for all humankind.

EQUALITY

Norm reminds us that equality is embedded into our country's foundational values as a democracy. Where the "golden door of freedom" means that every individual has the right to freedom, and ensuring this right is everyone's responsibility.

Norm: The golden door of freedom is not the door to Fort Knox in Kentucky, nor the key to Wall Street, nor shares in General Motors or U.S. Steel. That golden door speaks of a more elusive concept, one of a democracy, that all people are free and equal, and that every person has a soul which must be accounted for. That each one of us is responsible when one of us goes to prison, that each of us, for that matter, is responsible when one of us makes good. That when one of us dies, all of us die a little because we are all humankind.

LOVE

Transcending all is Norm's desire for spreading "agape" love. This type of love is known as charitable and universal—the love for strangers, nature, or God. It embraces altruism—the unselfish concern for the welfare of others.

Norm: We have all heard that "love conquers all," though we probably don't all think about what that means in our lives. Even in the blindness of our outrage and anxiety of the nation and world today, we can find comfort believing that love, not hate, makes our world go around.

Love does not gain from reaction. Love is pro-action. Love sloughs off hate, anger, and a thousand other slurs that are part of the action/reaction formula. The problem is we do not often acknowledge the love in the world, nor do we understand how evil can even co-exist in this equation. Love is a much harder act to follow through on than the easier reaction with instruments of revenge and hate.

THE WORLD TODAY

A growing sense of uneasiness, especially after the shocking 9/11 bombings on U.S. soil, led Norm to begin writing life lessons to pass down to his grandchildren. His intention was to plant the seeds of everlasting hope and ground them to be effective leaders of their lives and in the world around them.

After his cancer diagnosis, the life lessons he'd written for his grandchildren weren't enough to counter the alarming polarization in our country and world. As we watched news stations become partisan, and truth become harder to find, I pressed the record button and asked Norm to give us perspective on how the world had come to where it is today.

> *Norm:* The world is indeed in travail but no more than in times past. After centuries of fighting inequality and vying for justice, we haven't succeeded very well. We are still fighting the battle for peace and equality.
>
> Our divisions today demonstrate the seeming impossibility of humans to be a friend to their own kind. One has only to look at the events in the world around us to know that there are forces which seek to destroy rather than build.
>
> Extreme views have emerged and are a necessary corrective to human frailty and error, but seldom do such views advance doable and realizable solutions for making progress toward a better world. When public spirit wanes, we are prone to fall prey to the absolutist's leadership. We've stopped listening to one another, being open minded. Me first is the slogan of our time.
>
> It seems we have a lesson or two left to learn, namely that we have to be vigilant in our fight for truth and righteousness. When the world has all but lost the power to understand itself, then the seeds for revolution have been planted. These are action times.

VALUES-INFUSED LEADERSHIP

A moral code of values was embedded in Norm's genetic makeup. He knew that values were the common denominator for capable leadership.

One early morning I found Norm in the den, reading the Book of Daniel. When he asked if I had read it, I was honest and told him I had not. Always taking advantage of a learning opportunity, he told me we'd talk about it after I finished reading. Once done, we began exploring his ideas to reintegrate ethical and moral "norms" into a meaningful mythology fit for our times. Norm used the example of Daniel, and urges us to do the same—demand more of our leaders and ourselves—politician after politician, citizen after citizen. Once again, I hit the record button.

> *Norm:* I've been asking God, What in the world are you doing? You know we need a different kind of leadership. How do I cope when I have no confidence in my leaders? I have to ask because I'm one of the owners of the corporation (the United States). I vote. Where is the ethical and moral fiber in our society which would have made Russian interference in our democratic elections unthinkable if not impossible?
>
> I've been rereading the Book of Daniel because of the current political situation. It's an analysis of humankind and our inability to do the right things consistently. It demonstrates that when we build our leaders with feet of clay, they're sure to fall. If you drop a rock on their feet, they'll break. Many of our leaders today mimic the king with feet of clay.
>
> We must choose leaders that are grounded in rock solid values, who live and work for the welfare of all people. We can't keep electing people to office who have no concept of a unifying mission and have humongous egos, many seeking power for power's sake or a way to get rich. A leader of a country that ignores values like honesty, integrity, trustworthiness, and love does so at that nation's own peril.
>
> We must also ask: Where are the followers who would live and work for others? Where are our servant leaders?

Those who navigate differences to unify the people? Those with courage to make changes when needed and for sticking things out when the going gets tough.

There are no quick answers. We must get away from the idea that only one of us is right. If we want to know the answer to questions, we have to be able to face the questions down. Talk them through, think them through, wrestle them through. Bring them to problem solving situations where you can learn what's going on, what isn't going on, make changes. We must consider ideas and views of others as we plot and plod our course. We need leaders who don't think they know all the answers, so we can get away from the idea that only one of us is right.

WHERE WE BEGIN: NORM'S MESSAGE TO US ALL

In our last conversation, Norm and I turned off the recorder and I stopped taking notes. Dusk was settling in, and there were no distractions as I listened closely to the message he wanted to leave with us. His twinkling blue eyes conveyed the surety of what he knew to be true, that it's up to us to live our best lives every day. That we need to expect more of ourselves. We need to care for one another. And that when we unleash this goodness, the reward is joy.

Norm's secret to a life well lived was simple. Really simple. Open your heart to seeing the world as one family. Envision peace without war. Then begin by evaluating yourself and what you stand for. Define, redefine, or recommit to your values. Live them every day, taking them everywhere you go. Then live to help another. Then another. Lose your ego if it's getting in the way. Unity begins in our hearts.

Norm's message is not about one right way to live. Each of us has our own set of values, experiences, and knowledge that are not necessarily transferable to another person. Nor did he want this book to be about politics or one particular faith. It's about what is possible when people live by a similar moral rulebook.

The chapters that follow tell the story of Norm. They also illustrate the influence of a father on a daughter, and why he asked me to finish writing this book. Along the way, I realized I've been walking in his footsteps. He knew my heart was already committed to carrying on his legacy. In sharing his voice, I discovered my own. The hope is that you will find inspiration to make changes in your own story.

At the end of our final conversation, Norm knew he'd done everything in his power to prepare those he was leaving behind. It's all found in the pages of this book. The rest is up to us.

I believe that if he'd lived to end this story, he'd tell us, as his father told him, "We cannot stand idly by."

SEARCH FOR WHAT YOU CAN PUT INTO LIFE,
NOT WHAT YOU GET OUT OF IT.

Norm

—DR. NORMAN D. FINTEL

PART I

The Planting Season

1925–1958

CHAPTER 1

Tilling the Soil

HERITAGE AND FAMILY VALUES (1925–1930)

WHAT A CHILD SEES, HE BECOMES.

—WALT WHITMAN

NOT ALL OF US ARE FORTUNATE with the circumstances of our birth. We don't get a say in how we enter the world. And we enter unblemished before circumstances seep into our beings.

The genes we inherit, the home and family we are born into, the community that surrounds us—all these are a part of us. They shape our ways of understanding and interacting with the emerging world of people and events. These circumstances influence what we do at those exact moments where life choices are before us; where an instant can change the story of our lives. We are all always in the process of becoming, and nothing that touches us leaves us untouched. No matter how we begin life, we all get to have a say in how we choose to live the life we've been given.

For my father, Norm Fintel, this process of becoming began when family, heritage, faith, and farming converged, embedding a remarkable combination of values that were seemingly passed down in the genetic makeup of the Fintel family. It began on a farm in Nebraska, where early settlers plowed and enriched the soil, and where the seeds of his character were planted, along with the imperative to do things right. His parents nurtured in him an open mind, giving him the freedom to explore and discover the person he was meant to be. These seeds, nourished over his lifetime, took root and would spread bounty to multitudes.

It begins on a farm in the late 1920s and early '30s, a brutal time for the country with the Great Depression and Dust Bowl etching scars into many souls. Somehow, Norm escaped these ravages, and at some point in his earliest years, a light appeared and became his beacon.

Beginning before he was cognitively aware of what was shaping his life, my father's path was headed to where the sources of truth and wisdom prevailed. The immeasurable influence of the circumstances of his birth put him on the Autobahn to his future.

FAMILY

Over his lifetime, Norm put pen to paper, recording his early experiences. His story is best told in his own words and begins with his most profound influence—his family.

> *Norm:* I want to stress how important family life and ties are for one growing up. As is so often the case, we really don't understand things as they happen to us. It is only later that the whole pattern begins to take shape and make some sense. This was the case for me.
>
> My story begins in 1925, born in Monrovia, California,

the son of Ernest and Nora Koester Fintel. Two years earlier, my father and mother had picked up their meager belongings from their farm in Nebraska and, with my older sister Eileen, took the train to California to seek improved health and work for my dad.

We returned to Nebraska when my sister Margaret was a newborn and I was three, because mom and dad wanted to go home. Dad had largely regained his health but not enough to give him confidence to return to farming. Instead, he bought a pool hall in very rural Byron, Nebraska, (population 200). He did well, charging just nickels and dimes for beers and cigars. You could play pool for a dime.

After three years, making quite a little money, my dad still had farming in his blood. He returned to the farm his father had purchased one mile north of Deshler—a metropolis of 1,177 people, most of whom worked in a local broom factory.

Farm families were large. My mom had seven brothers and one sister. My dad had four brothers and two sisters. These sixteen provided twenty-seven offspring. Two of the sixteen, my mother and father, counted the four of us (including my sisters Eileen, Margaret, and Gert), and then we four added a total of seventeen grandchildren.

We were not a family that did a lot of hugging and kissing. Not that we didn't love each other; it just wasn't the way of our people. Love was shown in all sorts of ways but seldom spoken.

A GERMAN HERITAGE

When I read my father's stories about the "way of our people," I realized where my own stoicism originated, as well as some of my other irritating traits. The influence of his German Lutheran heritage cannot be understated, nor can the ramifications of German immigrants that settled in his home state of Nebraska. It was a heritage that valued hard work, honesty, moral leadership, excellence, and deep faith.

> *Norm:* What has shaped me? Let's start at the beginning with my grandfather, William von Fintel, a German immigrant. In 1888, at the age of fourteen, he came to the U.S. by himself with only one dollar to his name, speaking no English—all to escape the draft into Kaiser's army. His parents had encouraged him.

There is no doubt that a brave, pioneering spirit was alive in my great grandfather, William von Fintel. Or that it was passed down to the next generation and the next. Pioneers shake up the status quo and have a vision of something better beyond their immediate world and ways. They take responsibility for their own lives and futures. This dogged determination, sometimes called stubbornness, was passed along to my father, and I can see it in my own life as well.

> *Norm:* My grandfather William went to work on farms, eventually settling in Thayer County, Nebraska. He was a shrewd businessman, typically German. Ruthless. You did it right or you didn't do it. Through hard work, he became a wealthy man and ended up owning nine farms, maybe ten. He and many others like him not only had material successes, but they and succeeding generations of men and women truly were "giants in the earth." God-fearing, law-respecting, industrious, and quite pragmatic.
>
> There were Germans all over. More than to any other country in the world, they came here. Sixty-five percent of all immigrants at one time were from Germany, so you got the best of Germany fleeing. As with all refugee crises, we ought to take them all in and say, *Welcome, let's help you make it.* They only wanted a better life.

BORN INTO LOVE

Being born into this special family gave Norm a running start in life. He was born into love with parents who taught by example. The twinkle in Grandpa's eye whenever he spoke with Grandma set an example of family harmony that's hard to duplicate. I saw the same spark in my father's eye when he would connect with my mom. I was in my mid-twenties before I realized that not all parents were like mine.

> *Norm:* Neither my mother nor my father had a prescription for life. Ours was not a life of wealth and ease. Most of what I call "life preparation" came from having to do things for ourselves and for others. My parents were morally upright and hard working. I have no one but myself to blame for procrastination and laziness, or for lapses of any other of the virtues.
>
> We were not a demonstrative family, but we were a solid, loving family in which conversation about life and its duties and hopes was mostly left for us to discern for ourselves. In a way, we didn't have to speak our feelings—we sensed them and returned them.
>
> As my sisters—Eileen, Margaret, and Gert—and I grew older, we began to experience and later to realize that my parents were very much in love. My mom's love was the quiet kind. My dad was more open and explicit, and it sometimes was almost painful to us kids.
>
> My parents taught us by example rather than through many spoken words. Later, I know I failed many times to be such a silent teacher to my own children. My wife Jo and I chose to model the behavior for the most part, but don't ask our children if that really was true.

It was really true. There were no raised voices and few scolding words in my upbringing. That's not to say Peggy, Bill, and I didn't need them, especially me. Silence is a very effective form of discipline. With my own daughters, I did my best to model this hands-off parenting style and not indulge the "helicopter" style of today. Now, having read my father's many childhood stories, I've begun to rethink how I might make changes when helping to raise my grandchildren.

My father's mother, Nora, gave him the gift of exploration, a love of learning, and most importantly a library card. She passed along her enormous capacity for kindness, which I only hope to master one day. She nurtured an open mind, giving young Norm permission to think big thoughts, a quality that over his lifetime was the impetus for his reputation as "a thinking man." With her quiet strength, Nora gave her son the gift of seeing the world with no filters for the color of skin, gender, or any other reasons that too often become weapons to divide us.

> *Norm:* I learned from my mother that quiet gentleness is a form of strength. She was quiet and kind. I have tried all my life to be like that— less successfully, I hasten to add.
>
> My mother saw to it that I was exposed to all kinds of ideas and duties. Having three sisters did not excuse me from household chores, like cooking, sweeping, and dusting. The girls made fun of me when I sat on the piano stool and mopped the floor with a long-handled dust mop. My mom said little so long as I got the job done. Looking back, she must have been a saint to put up with me and my penchant for teasing the girls.
>
> Because of my mother, I became a reader. She loved books. I loved books. She saw to it that I got a Deshler Library card. I would go on Saturdays and pick out books that I liked. I read all of the Horatio Alger books, the *X Bar X Boys* series, the *Elsie Dinsmore* series, *Black Beauty*, and everything of that nature I could find.
>
> I found the Horatio Alger books especially inspiring and gloried in the accomplishments of the young lads

> who fought for the right to do things and were rewarded by becoming millionaires. Alger captured the "spirit of America," opening my mind to the idea that I could make my life take any shape I wanted. At the time, I dreamed of making it in the world of business—even to becoming president of the USA, like Abraham Lincoln.

Horatio Alger was a 19th century author best known for his rags-to-riches stories about impoverished boys rising up through hard work, determination, courage, and honesty. Right up my father's alley.

NORM'S LIFE LESSON #1

LOVE IS KIND. NORA TAUGHT HER SON NOT TO JUDGE OTHERS AND TO LOOK FOR THE GOOD IN EVERYONE. ONE OF NORM'S FAVORITE ADAGES WAS "YOU GET MORE FLIES WITH HONEY THAN VINEGAR."

His mom's influence combined with that of his father—Ernie, as everyone called his dad—was a potent mix. Together they plowed and cultivated a fertile field as the base for Norm's morality and lifelong code of values. Teaching by example, Ernie instilled an unrivaled work ethic and was a model for taking pride for doing things right, "the way they ought to be done." He was forward-thinking and taught his son that leadership begins in the heart.

Like his father, Norm was always at heart a farmer. Farming shaped his entire life. He was always working the soil, planting seeds, and coaxing the most abundant plantings to fruition. Weeding was second nature to him, and even in his last days, he couldn't pass by a flowerbed without stopping to pull the weeds.

Norm: Dad, as you might guess, was a remarkable man. He was a farmer's farmer. A superior farmer. He worked harder than anybody else and never slowed down.

I learned a great deal from him. Mostly about honesty, good work habits, and meticulous attention to doing it right—the first time. He didn't stop and say, *Now hear this...* I learned from watching, trying, and then having him suggest ways to improve.

He taught me how to work. Not just *work* work but the effective, efficient use of energy that is directed toward achieving some long or short-term goals. He never talked of goals and wouldn't have understood modern day management terminology. He didn't need to understand—it was just a part of his makeup. The farmyard was always in order, and his machinery always repaired and ready by the start of each new season.

He took great pride in plowing a straight furrow. Many of our fields had rows a half-mile long. When plowing and planting, straight rows were important or you'd end up with short rows on the far side of the field. My dad's rows of corn were so straight, the neighbors said they could shoot a rifle down the middle and never hit a thing. Half a mile long and not a kink anywhere for forty or fifty acres. Learning how to plow a straight furrow was tough work, not my idea of fun, but knowing not only how but that it could be done, gave me a jump on others who were fearful of trying any new or difficult task.

He was equally meticulous about keeping the weeds out of his corn fields, which at their peak growing time were a thing of beauty.

He was fair and highly respected. *Honesty* and *integrity* are two words he often used. I learned these when he insisted on a handshake to take or close a deal. It was his bond, and he would not default. I was imbued with the desire and skill to do things right for moral and ethical reasons. Tenacity and skill alone might not always be enough, but they were a part of our witness to the world. Quite often, I wish I'd told him of my present great appreciation, but, of course, callow youth finds it hard to be grateful!

Once in a while, he'd lose patience with me when I got lost in a book. If I was assigned a job that involved some down time, I would inevitably pull a book out of the bib pocket of my overalls and disappear in the pages until he found me and read me the riot act. But he never banned the books. It was hard for him to understand my interest in books, in school, in religion, in reading the papers and listening to radio, but I also think he understood that I marched to a somewhat different drummer than him.

NORM'S LIFE LESSON #2

IF YOU ALWAYS TELL THE TRUTH, YOU NEVER HAVE TO REMEMBER WHAT YOU SAID. YOUR WORD IS YOUR BOND.

Perhaps the most significant value I learned from my father, and he from his father Ernie, was to think forward into the future, beyond how things are to how they could be. How to welcome change into everyday life. I see now that this lesson from my father, handed down from his father, shaped the way I approached my life and work. Thinking creatively and strategically is entertainment for the brain, something my father and I would relish over the course of our lives, especially for me in my career-building years.

A most potent example of my grandfather's innate ability to envision the future is demonstrated when the Dust Bowl hit during the 1930s, and the extreme weather obliterated crops. Instead of waiting for better weather and replanting like his neighboring farmers, Ernie looked for a better solution, boldly planting a new drought-resistant hybrid seed corn.

> *Norm:* There were some earth-shaking changes when I was very young. Many new inventions. The automobile and electric lights. The radio and television. Paved roads opened up a whole new world for all of us. The most memorable invention that showed my dad's innovative spirit was when he decided to plant a new hybrid seed corn.
>
> I was in the kitchen when Dad complained that some of our neighbors thought it was a mistake to adopt this new-fangled idea. He was disturbed and told my mom that other farmers were saying it was not a good idea. They gave all sorts of reasons such as, "Too hard, the hogs and cattle won't eat it," or "It would be too hard on the land." Their rationalizations bothered my dad. I suppose he was a bit worried they might be right.
>
> By midsummer the story began to change. The hybrid corn grew a foot taller. It had two ears per stalk instead of the usual one. Its yield, even on a relatively dry year in Nebraska, was twenty-five per cent higher at forty bushels per acre. It was greener, taller, and better at standing up to insects, wind, and rain storms. Needless to say, my dad began to plant nothing but hybrid seed. Other farmers followed only after witnessing results, and even then, it took years.

As children, we don't always realize or appreciate our parents' wisdom. The realization of his father's innovative spirit would surface thirty years later when Norm was in a master's program at the University of Wisconsin. There he heard two Iowa State Agriculture professors present a paper on the early adoption of new ideas, citing the example of the reluctance of American farmers to plant hybrid seed corn in the 1930s. Norm's respect for his father rose, as it became clear that Ernie, an early adopter, modeled the innovative leadership now being discussed by his professors.

NORM'S LIFE LESSON #3

BE WILLING TO LISTEN TO NEW IDEAS, EVEN WHEN YOUR FIRST REACTION IS, *NO, NOT RIGHT NOW.* CHANGE IS A GUARANTEE IN LIFE. EXPECT IT, ENCOURAGE IT, LEVERAGE IT: YOU MUST LEARN FROM IT AND INNOVATE. RADICAL CHANGE COMES SLOWLY. AS NORM OFTEN SAID, "NOW WE'RE COOKING WITH GAS."

One final example of his father's enormous lifelong influence is revealed in a story about the importance of taking action and doing what's right.

> *Norm:* From my dad, I learned how to get things done. I remember when it first happened. I was maybe ten. We were watching a hub barn being built. I was looking around and observing what people were doing when he said, "Don't just stand there, do something. Pick up a board and do something yourself."

He never told me what to do. Just to do something. I've been grateful for that ever since.

NORM'S LIFE LESSON #4

ACT WITHOUT BEING ASKED. MOST IMPORTANTLY, WORK CANNOT BE SEPARATED FROM THE WAY YOU ARE, ETHICALLY AND MORALLY.

EARLY HOME LIFE

Beyond the influence of his heritage, his family life and parents, life on a farm in Nebraska during the Great Depression and Dust Bowl of the 1930s shaped Norm in many ways. Despite the catastrophic economic fallout suffered by so many, farmers had the luxury of food on their tables. There is a lightness and feeling of comfort in my father's descriptions of his early home life on the farm.

Norm: We lived in a frame house built in the 1890s. Downstairs there was a kitchen, dining/living room, parlor, and guest bedroom, and upstairs there were four large bedrooms. The center bedroom was the only one with heat, vented from the kitchen below. When we were very young, all four of us children slept in the same bed, next to my parents' bed, in that single bedroom.

When I was older, I had my own bedroom which was not insulated. On the frigid, cold nights, we put heavy flat irons in the oven, then when heated, wrapped them in towels and put them by our feet. We had "feather beds," called comforters today. The really good ones were stuffed with down from ducks or geese. These were put over two or three blankets, so once you got the bed warmed up, you had good sleeping. Of course, getting up in the cold meant we grabbed our clothes to dress by the heating stove in the dining room. We had a "thunder pot" for relief, but morning constitutionals meant a trip outdoors to the outhouse. In retrospect, I can see that ignorance was a bit blissful.

Since the kitchen was almost always heated, it was where we lived most of the time. The range burned dry corn cobs and wood. We filled a "reservoir" water tank every day that circulated around the oven and heated the water used for cooking and for our wash stand where we scrubbed up before a meal. Drinking water was carried in by pail from the windmill.

There wasn't a lot of privacy. The old galvanized tub was brought in from the laundry house and put in the middle of the kitchen for bathing right in front of the stove, which was nice in the winter!

We did not have electricity, so we did not have fans or air conditioning. Summer heat waves meant temperatures in the 90s to 100 plus. The uninsulated house built up and maintained its heat level deep into the night, making for sweltering sleep. I often pulled my bed in front of the one window of my bedroom and hoped for any breeze to cool me down.

NORM'S LIFE LESSON #5

"HOME IS A PLACE THAT WHEN YOU GOTTA GO THERE, THEY GOTTA LET YOU IN."

THE LUTHERAN FAITH

Beyond the comfort of his home, another source of comfort was Norm's deep Lutheran faith which steadied him throughout his life—like a thousand-pound anchor. Though he didn't wear it on his sleeve, you could sense it when you were in his presence.

Norm: With so many German settlers in Nebraska, small towns grew up and so did Lutheran churches. In my town, there were two Lutheran churches with 600 members each, and we only had a thousand in town.

It's fair to say that my faith shaped all of the major decisions in my lifetime—in unknowing ways sometimes, sometimes clear and sometimes not. When you have an over-arching goal to be of service, as I would later find out I did, that changes things.

Our family, like ninety percent of all families of our day, went to church and tried to live a good life, living according to the Ten Commandments. My parents had a simple piety. That is, there was not a long list of do's and don'ts—especially the don'ts. Piety was not worn as a garb but was valued as an inner quality.

Today, Lutherans are one of the largest denominations of Protestantism. Two principal beliefs guided Norm's life, as did the boldness of the shake-it-up leadership of Protestant reformer Martin Luther.

> *Norm:* In the 16th century, Martin Luther, a monk, professor, and reformer, shook things up. With a Ph.D. at twenty-four, fluent in Greek, Hebrew, and Latin, he asserted that the Bible is central to religious authority, and that people are saved by their faith and not by their deeds. And that good deeds come from having faith.
>
> Another one of Luther's key beliefs that influenced my entire life was this business of faith and vocation. Lutherans live by a sense of calling, an overarching goal to be of service. Our task is to find a vocation, a calling, whatever that may be. I might be a storekeeper, but I still have a calling.
>
> Martin Luther irrevocably changed the direction of the Church in 1517 when he saw that indulgences were being sold by priests as a way for people to redeem their souls—like buying forgiveness in a package. He said, *This is no way to run a church,* and famously nailed his Ninety-Five Theses on a door of a church, calling for change and sparking the Protestant Reformation.

I can't remember how many times I heard my father say, "If you are going to sin, sin boldly," words he attributed to Luther. Or "Act now and ask for forgiveness later." No doubt, Luther combined with Ernie were the early impetus for Norm's leadership proclivity for stirring the pot to move things forward. Until learning about these major influences in my father's life, I never thought about why I had questioned and challenged the status quo—sometimes annoyingly so.

This indoctrination into Lutheran tenets set Norm on an early path for determining his vocation, his life's calling. Through our interviews and reading his many stories, I've searched for when he became cognizant of the defining moments in his early development. Did they happen before he was old enough to be aware of them, or did they spring up from a more rational theory, based on experiences when he was in his teens? This theory is explored in stories about his development as a child, the subject of the next chapter.

QUESTIONS FOR SELF-REFLECTION

- Each of us was born into circumstances beyond our choosing. What were these for you? Both positive and not-so-positive.
- For parents and grandparents, what values define you? What steps did you take to instill these in your children? What more could you do?
- Do you think change is best to be avoided or embraced? Can you think of a change you've made recently?
- If you see someone you don't know in distress, for example, crying in a grocery store or sitting alone at a school cafeteria, how do you react?

CHAPTER 2

Planting Seeds

EARLY INFLUENCES
(1930–1943)

GIVE ME A PLACE TO STAND,
AND I SHALL MOVE THE EARTH.
—ARCHIMEDES

REFLECTING BACK ON HIS EARLY YEARS OF CHILDHOOD, Norm often spoke of being "a hole waiting to be filled." The open mind and heart nurtured by his parents gave him an insatiable curiosity for all that was the unknown. Like a sponge in water, he absorbed his surroundings as he explored, read every book in sight, and observed the ways of the world that surrounded him. This included the stock market crash of the Great Depression and the mass exodus of Midwest farmers during the brutal, barren years of the Dust Bowl.

As the only son to help in the fields, Norm was often found with his nose in a book or burrowed into a bale of hay, gazing at the sky and mesmerized by the changing shape of the clouds. These habits lasted a lifetime as his eternal quest for knowledge and truth kept filling that never-ending hole, keeping him always hungry for more.

The one-room schools he attended allowed him to stretch to higher levels of thinking and learning. By the age of ten, when prejudice against people of color seemed an excuse for some to ignore the *Golden Rule*, he took a stand for racial justice. When he was in his teens, a pastor would sense a presence in him and plant a seed for an everlasting bloom, giving him what my father later called "mental breathing room."

In this chapter, we'll look at those many influences that shaped him during his childhood and two remarkable defining moments that altered the course of his life.

LIFE ON THE FARM

The hard-work factor of farming makes me appreciative of my convenient scrambled eggs, strip of bacon, and glass of cold milk. For so many today, we are removed from what transpires in the farm-to-table process. Here's a look at an average day in the life of a farm boy and the life-long values embedded into all Norm's subsequent years by his daily activities.

> *Norm:* When I grew up, ninety percent of America's labor force was in agriculture. Today the obverse is true.
>
> Farming is a life of hard work and hard play. Keeping a three-hundred-acre farm in good condition was a seven-days-a-week job. We had a herd of 25–35 cattle, raised about 100 hogs a year, and kept 500 laying hens.
>
> As I approached that magic age of ten, I got to do "chores," a euphemism for mostly un-fun things. Early on, I fed the chickens and gathered at least 250 eggs a week, because my sisters hated to stick their dainty hands under the setting hens.

I had to enter the hen house carefully and quietly, for if I made a sudden move on entry, the entire flock of 500 hens would fly into the air, creating a clatter and so much dust, I could hardly breathe. Breathing was even harder every Saturday morning when the cleaning of the manure under the chicken roost released the foulest ammonia odor one can imagine. We pitched the manure on a horse-drawn spreader and hauled it out to the grain fields for fertilizer. We tried to always drive into the wind, but…

The hogs were fun to watch. They could strip an ear of corn down to the cob in no time and lose few kernels, all the while doing it in the muck and mire only a hog lot can accumulate. Then it was up to us kids to get down there on reasonably dry days to pick up those stinking cobs. It wasn't much fun, except one day I threw a mostly dry cow pie at my sister Eileen. The trouble was my dad saw the act, and I paid the consequences. I remember the spanking, but I doubt that my body was as bloody and bruised as my psyche was.

Early on, we were taught how to milk cattle. At first, my dad or mom took the hard milkers and the kickers. It wasn't long before I inherited most of those. Each cow gave up to a pail of milk. First, we cleaned the udders. Then we sat on a low, T-shaped stool and held the pail between the knees with head butting into the cow's side as needed. To avoid being swatted by dirty tails, I took to pinning the long tail hairs between my knee and the pail—you really did not want that tail to swat you as it swatted flies!

One of the ways I combated boredom was to squirt milk from the teat directly into the open mouth of one of our twenty-seven barn cats waiting nearby. They got pretty good at lapping it up and then cleaning up their faces with tongue and paws.

Morning chores took at most an hour, and by the time we got back to the house the smell of fried eggs, fried potatoes, and ham or bacon made you forget any misgivings you had about a new day dawning. On rare occasions, my mother would cook up the cornmeal the night before and let it cool in a large crock. In the morning, the hardened mush was sliced and fried in bacon grease, and then eaten with butter and syrup. No one knew about cholesterol then. Nor did we know of anyone succumbing to its supposed threats.

Lunch was lighter, sometimes just sandwiches, leaving room for a twenty-minute nap on the hard, wooden floor before returning to the fields. During the long days of summer, we were in the fields by six in the morning and worked there until near sundown.

I learned to appreciate quiet time, uncluttered by the noises and people of today. In the fields, all you could hear was the plodding and grunting of the mules, the leathery squeak of the harness on the mules' collars, occasional groans from the machinery, the quick blasts of foul air from the hay burners, and an occasional "giddup" from my dad. To this day, I love the quiet times best.

I grew up on a farm right before the beginning of the mechanization of farm work. If all the innovations had been invented a few years earlier, I might still be a farmer. I still miss the soil, the growing seasons, and especially, the harvest of the crops.

THE GREAT DEPRESSION

The Great Depression of the 1930s hit in the midst of Norm's childhood. While he was somewhat sheltered living on a farm, the government's response carried ramifications lasting throughout my father's lifetime.

Norm: I remember my dad's great anxiety the day he came home from town to tell Mother that the bank had failed and we had lost all our money (later repaid at about 32 percent). Though the account was only in the hundreds of dollars, the very idea of failure was a heavy blow to their confidence in the system. It was just the beginning of nearly a decade of austerity—not poverty. We had no money, but we had our farm and its animals and resources, and we had food.

Life was simple, but it was good. My sisters and I were happy with what we had, not knowing we were poor. Nor did we know the severity of the economic crisis our nation was going through. Our happiness was not built on material things but on relationships and values carried by the family, the church, and the community. When disaster struck in our rural community, we learned that it's our responsibility to be a good neighbor to whomever is near us or within our reach. It takes but one good deed to spawn ten more.

NORM'S LIFE LESSON #6

BUILDING COMMUNITY NO MATTER WHERE YOU LIVE IS A VITAL RESOURCE FOR SUPPORT. THIS GIVE-AND-TAKE, SHARING HARDSHIPS, BUILDS FRIENDSHIP AND BELONGING. REACH OUT TO YOUR NEIGHBORS.

My father observed government's hand in the rural landscape as President Franklin D. Roosevelt, the only president to be elected to serve four terms, led efforts to stem the dreary tide of the Great Depression. The New Deal measures were not always popular.

Norm: I had observed enough of the hardships of the Depression years to know that in the long run, less government was better government. I knew my dad hated the New Deal because it forced him to come face-to-face with policies and programs he thought were an abomination. Some of the New Deal measures were a bit scandalous for the self-made farmers.

Farms had to have a "Roosevelt Monument," a free, rather deluxe, outdoor toilet, named in honor of our esteemed Depression president, Franklin Delano Roosevelt. Every farm and many homes in cities and towns had an outhouse—usually quite shabby and odorous. The new ones were well-built and solidly anchored in cement, but they still had two holes and a big smell when the wind was in your direction. Ours was northeast of the house, because winds from that quarter were few and far between, except on snowy winter days when the dung was frozen anyway.

Another unpopular New Deal measure was the government's order to slaughter hogs to bring up the price. My dad could not bring himself to dig a ditch and bury a hundred of our young pigs, so he and my mom arranged for barbecuing the young hogs, and then invited the poor people from all around to come and eat. It may have been an empty gesture, but it taught me that taking a direct shot at starvation was the better thing. He often said, "If you want something done right, do it yourself," which is exactly what he did by solving the government's hog slaughter order his own way.

EXTREME WEATHER: THE DUST BOWL, HAIL, AND TORNADOES

Coming on top of the Great Depression, the drought, dust, and extreme weather of the "Dirty Thirties" plagued farmers to no end.

Norm: Looking back on my childhood, it is not the negatives of those years that I remember. It is love of family and awe of the powers of the good earth. I am, at root, a farm boy.

Norm was better at predicting weather than any meteorologist. The Dust Bowl was a hard way to learn. The story is worth telling because this extreme weather, lasting for so many years, gave him a foundation of resilience, patience, and perseverance.

I don't remember my father ever being ruffled by stress. He was always able to stand back, see the bigger picture, and then find solutions. No doubt, the unpredictable, uncontrollable, and relentless weather ingrained in him an overriding sense of optimism. Weather didn't break Ernie or Norm, like it did so many.

> *Norm:* The crash of 1929 did not bother the farmers much until the Depression was coupled with a severe drought in 1933 and 1934.
>
> I learned how to read nature's signs by listening to my dad's conversation with my mother and with his neighbors. I knew it was important by the intensity of their concern and their voices.
>
> Any kind of south wind and a buildup of cumulus clouds would invariably trigger at least isolated storms, and when a front approached, there was a chance of severe weather—all the way from strong gales to hail and tornados.
>
> This was not the case during the drought years. Then, nature seemed to be conspiring to keep us perpetually praying for rain. Even storms were welcome, with all their hail and damaging winds, because any rain would help to replenish the Saharan earth and keep the prairie pastures green for the cattle.

During that time, a severe drought struck the Great Plains, and, coupled with farmers' failure to understand methods for preventing wind erosion of topsoil, more than 75 percent of soil was blown away by the end of the 1930s. Unanchored, it turned to dust, blackening the sky and often reducing visibility to three feet or less. It forced a third of the farmers to migrate west, driven out by heat and desolation they had never imagined possible. When all was said and done, more than 3.5 million people moved west to escape the Dust Bowl.

Norm: I remember the "Dirty Thirties" being so dry that when the winds blew, the dust would swirl into the air so high that it blocked the sun. These were years when my mother packed up the curtains and anything like them into sealed boxes, to be unpacked several years later when the drought and dust storms ended.

We had had almost no rain for three years. The crops were drying up. Prairie grasses almost disappeared, and the hot dry winds of summer almost made Nebraska and its neighboring states of Kansas, Oklahoma, and others into a desert.

We left country school more than once in the middle of the day because it was too dark to hold classes. My dad came to get us, I recall, and when we got home in mid-afternoon, the chickens had gone to roost. It was darker by far than any eclipse.

When the storms finally came, we worried about hail and tornadoes. The severe hail came in 1933, in 1935, and again in 1937. I remember the agony on my dad's face when we saw that the small grains had been pounded into the dirt, and the corn that minutes before had been two feet tall was now reduced to one-foot stumps, too damaged to recover in time for a crop.

Then came the tornadoes. When I was ten, my mother and we four children were in the barn milking the cows late one afternoon when a small squall line had built up. As my mother looked out, she said, "There's a tornado coming." Later, word came that the tornado had indeed struck, but not just anywhere. It had struck her family's farm where they lost everything except for a heavily damaged home.

I have often wondered why I did not fear storms, seeing the havoc they could create. I think it is because these storms were also about the only way of watering the arid land and the crops growing in it. Rain was a blessing. Every snowfall in winter was welcomed, even if the wind blew it into enormous drifts. To this day I am excited to watch a storm approaching, and then to hear the thunder and see its precursor, the lightning flashes, one of which once set our barn afire.

If adversity builds character, perhaps that is why so many farmers have character as well as faith. All the farmers I knew went to church every Sunday. They worked hard to have a good crop, but the vagaries of wind and weather often made their work of little use. The farmer's ego is constantly being tempered by the elements of nature, so year after year he goes on being the best farmer he can be, and trusts and has faith that God will provide the rest.

EDUCATION: THE LESSONS OF EQUALITY

Even though Norm's parents didn't attend high school, they saw change in the wind and understood the value of education and intellectual development. In these early years, faith and school often went hand in hand, and Norm was exposed to stretching his mind by listening to older students' lessons. Along with his mother's encouragement for learning, his teachers expanded his education far beyond the ABCs, and one special teacher opened his eyes to issues of faith and justice. It was during this time that he experienced the clarity of wisdom far above his years that embedded core values for the rest of his life.

Norm: I loved my one-room country schools and have never felt short-changed because I couldn't go to a larger, more exciting school. I believe the one-room concept was a good learning laboratory.

My first school was District 60. Dorothy Grundmann was a typical first year teacher who graduated from high school and after six weeks of Normal Training qualified for her certificate. There were thirteen students in eight grades, all learning their lessons in one room. Learning came not just in her teaching me, but in my observing and learning with each class and each subject as it came along.

In fifth grade, for reasons not entirely clear to me, my parents decided I should go to parochial Peace Lutheran School, another one-room school with about thirty students, fifth through eighth grade. Perhaps it was loyalty to the Church. Perhaps it was the high regard people had for the teacher, a man we called Professor Fred Scharmann.

I thought then that he was an old man from Germany—a typical classical educator and disciplinarian. His "spare the rod and spoil the child" approach seemed not to inhibit the free-spirited farm and small-town kids he taught. I know now that he was a fine teacher who gave me much more than the three R's.

To my delight, recess and lunch were totally unsupervised and so a time for mischief. One day we stuffed corn cobs into the exhaust pipe of a book salesman's car. We found a way to watch, without being obvious, until the car was started, and the cob would be sent sailing. If it was in firmly enough, the engine would backfire and create an even greater blast. There was something delicious about this skullduggery, and we would collapse with laughter, hoping we wouldn't get caught. I can see this behavior now in my grandsons and am reminded of how innocent their behavior really is, and of how conservative I have become.

Prof. Scharmann must have had a good ear for cadence and rhythm, and we were careful not to get too far out of line. Perhaps we stopped because we knew he kept a length of rubber hose behind the back door. My dad told me on the day I first went to Peace School that if I "got a lickin'" at school, I would get another at home. Most of us were reared by families like that. It had a lot to do with basic law and order.

It was Scharmann's Bible story critiques and lessons that shaped Norm's belief in equality. The lesson of being a Good Samaritan stuck. At the age of ten, without realizing it, a spark was lit for a lifetime committed to righting the wrongs resulting from any type of discrimination.

Norm: It wasn't any one thing. I remember when I was ten, watching a black man at the county fair. I'd never seen one before, and as I watched, I heard name calling and negative references. At that time, I didn't realize this was discrimination. I just thought, *Well, that's the way the world is.* But it didn't seem right.

There was a well-liked Mexican family in Deshler that lived in shanty town, in a hut across the tracks. The father worked for the railroad and had four or five kids that went to my school. We'd drive by, and I remember feeling sorry they had to live like that. I became aware of the inequities for the first time. This introduced me to classes of people. The son later became the superintendent of schools, and he was a great one, so it wasn't racism that I experienced. Little pieces kept coming up about what was right or wrong.

NORM'S LIFE LESSON #7

EVERYONE IS EQUAL. LOOK BEYOND WHAT MAKES US DIFFERENT. A GOOD SAMARITAN UNSELFISHLY HELPS OTHERS, ESPECIALLY STRANGERS. THE NEBRASKA STATE MOTTO IS "EQUALITY BEFORE THE LAW."

Norm's high school life was not overly memorable, except for seeing the impact of approaching World War II and for developing a relationship with a mentor who would change his life. My father would go on to pay it forward, mentoring thousands over his lifetime.

> *Norm:* I attended Deshler High School from 1941 to 1943. War news, blackouts, worry about friends being drafted and loved ones in the service all happened. To be sure, there were fun times and memorable games and events but always overshadowed by the grim reality of war!
>
> Our school started with 120 students, a total which was nearly halved by graduation time, after draft numbers were called and we began losing students.
>
> The upside of having fewer students was that doors were opened for me, being somewhat introverted, to explore more extracurricular activities. I sang in the choir and performed in a play. In shop class, I built a cedar chest from scratch that is still stored at son Bill's house for future generations to "marvel at."
>
> Sports interested me greatly—football, basketball, and track—I was able to win a place on the teams because so few students were attending—in football, for example, we had a squad of less than thirty. Each coach—we had a new one at least once each year—left a mark, but it was the last one, Wilmut Fruehling, who stuck with me and changed my life.

This mentor, Coach Fruehling, would reappear some years later in Norm's life (a tale for the next chapter) under pivotal, life-changing circumstances. But at this time in my father's life, he was developing an unwavering faith that guided his every step.

AN EARLY COMMITMENT TO SERVICE

The seeds of openness were sown early for my father by the words of Martin Luther and the influence of Pastor Fred Schwerin. And while Norm's personal faith journey greatly influenced his lifetime, he never made anyone feel it was "my way or the highway." His open spirit led to another life defining decision that once again shaped the values for his life.

> *Norm:* My early upbringing obviously had a strong impact on how I view faith, and how I feel it ought to be expressed and lived out in life. Faith is very personal, an internal guidance system with an externally charged battery that, like the Energizer Bunny, just keeps on keeping on.
>
> There was no magic moment for me. No sense of conversion. I learned from my parents, and from Pastor Schwerin and Professor Scharmann the openness of Lutheranism, absorbing that I was a part of something much larger than myself and the small world around me. No pressure really, just teaching by example that the values of faith were the essence of life.
>
> I suspect it was Pastor Fred Schwerin who had the most seminal impact on my religious outlook. It was he, in confirmation instruction and by example, who allowed for mental breathing room in such matters as the creation story and the examples he used from the life of Martin Luther, which carried the implied message of openness and faith.
>
> One day, Pastor Schwerin surprised me by challenging me to think beyond a life in Deshler to a life of service. He told me that I should think about being a pastor. I had not the slightest interest, but his suggestion that I had the qualities for the task gave me a bit of a start. He went on to say that I had the qualities of mind and spirit that it would take.
>
> I was shocked, and I don't think I even told my mother about it. He must have told my parents, because I recall a conversation about it—with no conclusions or pressure. But once inserted, this little hot spot never quite left me.

Whatever the circumstances and conversation, from that time forward it was not possible for me to avoid that vocation as one to be considered. At the time, I was certain I would never enter the profession, but the seed was planted, and it shaped what it meant to be a believer and how I was to do service in the world.

It was during these days that I consciously decided I would try to live a life of service. This was no small decision because I had cut my eye teeth on the Horatio Alger series and all sorts of other inspirational books for achievers. I knew I could be a millionaire or president of the United States if I set my mind to it. Naïve though that may have been, I can look back and see that I was not making conscious decisions, so much as I was being led by the spirit into a path of service.

My mind began probing for understanding of God and the world in which I now found myself. I read in the Bible the story of Solomon praying and God responding with, "Ask what you will, and I will give it to you." Solomon had prayed for wisdom and understanding so that he might carry out his heavy responsibility as king. God was so impressed that Solomon asked for these qualities and not for riches, power, and might, that God granted him not only wisdom and understanding but wealth as well.

From the story of Solomon, I learned to resort to prayer and meditation as a way of addressing my life's direction and the problems confronting me. It helped shape how I was to do service in the world. And like Solomon, praying for riches—like Horatio Alger—was not what I started asking for.

THE MOST SATISFYING THING IN LIFE IS TO HAVE BEEN ABLE TO GIVE A LARGE PART OF ONE'S SELF TO OTHERS.

—PIERRE TEILHARD DE CHARDIN

A PLACE TO STAND

My father had an early start zeroing in on the values that would define his life. I've tried imagining what it felt like for him to have a pastor sense a spiritual presence in him at such a young age of twelve. Or when he first felt that presence himself, and what it was like to then live his life so closely in touch with Spirit. He never talked about it with anyone, but I have no doubt he'd tell people that no matter what your age or what your life is about today, moving forward begins with looking inward.

> *Norm:* We are all shaped in ways that we cannot fully understand as we pass through the exposures and experiences of a life. I see my father and mother in me—how I work, how I react to others, how, indeed, I think.
>
> It takes a lifetime to recognize your very own "place to stand." While we build that platform from planks of knowledge and experience, the foundation has as its base our most deeply held values. My bedrock values formed early. Honesty, integrity, trustworthiness, and love are the values that built my platform. It's that place on which we stand with our lever and try to pry at least a small part of the world into something better than it was when we found it.
>
> *Who am I?* is the question of life. Your answer is the description of how you live out your life.

When Peggy, Bill, and I were young, we each hid our allowance money in one of Dad's books. My hiding place book, *Here I Stand* by Roland H. Bainton, was still on his shelves as we were writing this book. Of course, I searched it for money but found none, only to notice that the book's subject was a study on the life of Martin Luther, given to my father when he was in still college. Surely this is no coincidence, for he had found his place to stand early in life, committed to service and to the values that fueled that service. With his footing firmly on the path, his movement forward would initially consist of countless sputters and restarts as he maneuvered down the runway. But the doors continued to open for him as he searched for how to live his purpose, in ways appearing serendipitous at times but always spirit-led.

QUESTIONS FOR SELF-REFLECTION

- What core values would you say give you your "place to stand" in life?
- If you are a parent, how do you teach these values to your children?
- Do you think you treat people equally? Why or why not? What might you do differently?
- When you are faced with adversity, how do you react? If you could, would you change the way you react? How?
- Do you know your neighbors? If not, why not? Most of us don't live rurally, so how can we build a better sense of urban community?

CHAPTER 3

Windy Weather

SEARCH FOR PURPOSE, DOORS OPENING
(1943–1947)

THIS ABOVE ALL, TO THINE OWN SELF BE TRUE;
THOU CANST NOT THEN BE FALSE TO ANY MAN.
—WILLIAM SHAKESPEARE, *HAMLET*

WITH A MONUMENTAL DECISION MADE TO LEAD A LIFE OF SERVICE, Norm spent his late teens and early twenties trying to figure out what this meant. He had no plan. He let himself blow with the wind, going down backroads and taking a few detours along the way—all at the same time as our country and the world were experiencing their own growing pains.

War continued to escalate after the U.S. entry into WWII following Japan's attack on Pearl Harbor on December 7, 1941. Our forces joining allies on D-Day—June 6, 1944—to storm the beaches in Normandy and liberate Paris.

Later, when President Roosevelt died suddenly on April 12, 1945, Vice President Truman took over the highest office, and in what would become the last stages of the war, the U.S. dropped atomic bombs on Hiroshima and Nagasaki in August of 1945. The end of WWII found the world in utter turmoil, and to try to prevent future conflicts, the United Nations was created as the nations of the world searched for harmony.

The country took a step forward toward equality when Truman ended military segregation. Then the Brooklyn Dodgers drafted Jackie Robinson, the first black baseball player, lifting (and for a few, *disturbing*) the spirit of the nation.

All these issues were brewing as Norm was in his final year of high school and began searching for what it meant to live a life of service. He sputtered and restarted several times until a shocking event would capture his attention at the age of twenty-one. He learned that when opportunity knocks, you open the door and step in.

OPENING DOORS

As Nebraska and the Midwest emerged from a decade of drought and dust, the rains seemed to nurture my father's spiritual journey as well as the soil. His world expanded beyond the farm as he explored his decision to live a life of service.

He often experienced what he called *serendipitous moments*—those times, events, and circumstances that appear to have no particular logic, preparation, or prescience. Yet in retrospect, they were pivotal moments in his life. That story is best told in his own words, starting with his thoughts on searching for his purpose.

> *Norm:* All of us need time and space to let the spirit breathe in and through us, and help us become all that we can be. Life is like a series of hills and valleys. You go up and down, and up and down without recognizing the patterns. It could be because we like the road we are on and where

we are going, but it is just as likely that we are simply in gear and moving, and that seems like the thing to do.

We humans are destined to be searching. Not to search means that each day we kill a bit of the spirit within. Progress is not our goal. The pursuit is for the prize of understanding and appreciation both for what is and what may still be. Understanding comes slowly as the impact of ideas and information opens our minds to new ideas and new horizons.

Sometimes the doors opened, and if they didn't open, then I guess I wasn't supposed to do that. But when they did open, it wasn't because I was so smart; they opened because there was work that needed to be done and somebody's got to do it.

NORM'S LIFE LESSON #8

BE OPEN. WALK THROUGH OPEN DOORS EVEN WHEN YOU DON'T KNOW WHERE THEY MIGHT LEAD. TAKE FULL ADVANTAGE OF OPPORTUNITIES.

In his senior year of high school, Norm began probing for knowledge and understanding of the ramifications of dedicating his life to serving others.

Norm: In my last years of high school, it was the Luther League that further shaped my thinking about living a life of service. This young people's organization was about the only show in town after the weekend movies and an occasional dance at one of the pavilions.

I entered the League as an unthinking member. I listened carefully and took it all in. I was younger than most of the 150 others in attendance and green as grass.

When I look back on this, I can see no evidence that I was fitted for leadership. But there I was, elected as president of our chapter, and later serving as Federation President and a member of the International Luther League.

I was profoundly impressed by the charismatic leadership of Dr. Marcus Rieke, head of the International Luther League. His power was in his dedication to us as the future of the Lutheran Church and to the new ideas sweeping the Church as well as the country. Having been raised to welcome change and innovation, these new ideas lured me in, and I was hooked.

I realized that my faith had been shallow and immature. When I returned home after meeting, I remember telling my mother that something spiritual had happened, something deep and lasting. My philosophy became consciously based in faith, shaping all my major decisions, sometimes in unknowing ways, sometimes clear and sometimes not.

I still was not ready to commit to the ministry, though service remained my aim. I guess it is fair to say that I was not yet on my career path, but the door leading me to that path opened wider through my experience with the Luther League.

NORM'S LIFE LESSON #9

SEEK TRUTH THROUGH A HIGHER POWER.

A SOLID BELIEF SYSTEM MUST UNDERPIN YOUR VALUES.

HAVE FAITH TO BE GUIDED FROM WITHIN.

MILITARY LIFE

Norm was still in high school when WWII broke out. Beginning at age sixteen, he struggled with the need to raise crops and the need to serve his country. A boyhood reverence for Charles

Lindberg and his historic flight across the Atlantic Ocean at age 25 was rekindled when military jets zoomed close to home.

Norm: As I walked out of the local movie theatre on December 7, 1941, I heard about Pearl Harbor. Up until then, war was a distant event, now brought home with a vengeance. Our family shared the indignant feeling of all Americans.

At this time in my life, it is hard to visualize just how the events and people of the years after 1941 changed my life and the lives of all those around me. It was like being thrown into deep water and not knowing how to swim. Soon we were dealing with rationing, food stamps, blackouts, and the invasion of B-24 training airports nearby with great numbers of bombers doing training runs at low levels over our homes.

My interest in flying grew. I suspect the memory of Lindberg's flight was one of those factors which led me to want to fly. Even my high school mates knew that and predicted I would be an airline captain one day. They missed that prediction but not the fact that an airplane would influence my life.

After graduating high school in May 1943, I went to work on the farm. I was deferred from serving to help my dad with the heavy work of cultivating and raising crops. I began to realize that I needed to be with my classmates scattered around the world in the military service. I talked to my dad and told him of my dilemma. He understood, and I volunteered to be drafted into the US Army Air Corps Cadet training program in February 1944.

Going into the Army Air Corps even for a short eighteen months was an eye-opening experience for a green Nebraska farm boy. I learned a lot from a lot of people. What to do. What not to do. I learned lots of things they never talked about at church or on the farm. We were fed SOS (sh** on a shingle), not exactly biscuits and gravy.

It was in the Army when the change was made from pronouncing my last name *Fin*tel, with accent on first syllable, to Fin*tel*, with accent on the last syllable. This was because my staff sergeant. would call roll and say Fin*tel*, and I'd say, No, it's *Fin*tel. But he says, You're Fin*tel*, so from then on, I was Fin*tel*.

On D-Day, June 6, 1944, the sergeant pulled our troop together at 11 a.m. to tell us of the Normandy Beach landing and to lead us in a brief moment of silence. He made it clear we all needed to be ready for combat regardless of the outcome of that landing. I sat for the next 13 months, waiting to go to advanced training, but it never happened.

In November, after the war ended with the armistice on August 15, 1945, V-J day (Victory over Japan), I was offered a choice. Three more years or a quick discharge. I had seen enough of the military, and so I came home and got on with my life.

Not a great story, but no regrets either!

A WINNING TICKET

What happened next might seem like luck, and certainly luck followed my father through his life. Maybe it was serendipity, but if we dig deeper, a greater power was at work, changing the haphazard trajectory of his life, placing him on the right road for determining how he was to serve the world. It was a wake-up call that few of us can imagine, and that none of us could ignore.

Norm: Even upon discharge, my life was not directed by conscious decisions to go this way or that. What do you do in a small town in Nebraska in the winter?

So, I thought, they've got this GI bill which will pay for your tuition and give you something for room and board—$50 a month. Since I'd always been interested in writing, I enrolled as a pre-journalism major at the University of Nebraska. I'd done some writing for the local newspapers and the news and columns in high school, so it seemed like a good choice.

My determination not to be trapped into being a farmer disappointed my father. Before the machine-aided, business farming of later decades, I worked hard and had almost constant lower back pain, so the thought of continuous hard labor did not appeal to me.

I spent the first term at college in moderate study with a major in card playing and partying. I didn't exactly set the academic world on fire, but I had a good time and was moving along like Alice in Wonderland on a road that must lead somewhere. I was happy enough, intending to return in the fall, but I now know that I was not fulfilled.

NORM'S LIFE LESSON #10

"WHAT GOOD IS A HALF-BAKED POTATO?"

The lifestyle I'd fallen into at the university and my lack of certainty about my major in journalism were both on my mind when I went home in the summer to work the farm with my dad. I planned to return to the university in September. All that was soon to change.

I did not know then what was happening on July 4, 1946, but that day and the events that followed changed my life. I had been going along on a sidetrack and then what happened put me on the mainline track, all in the twinkling of any eye.

That day, July 4, 1946, begins my recollections that something more than good decision-making was responsible for my career path and advancement. Even this I did not see until many years later, as I recognized that most of the pivotal points in my life had no conscious decision base. Serendipity is an inadequate explanation. For me, the key was more like Spirit-led.

Deshler town life had a pattern of farmers and their families coming to town on Wednesday and Saturday nights for shopping and gossip. On one of those early summer nights, Eddie Buntemeyer, who worked in his dad's liquor store, came out front and greeted me. I didn't frequent the place much because of the cost, but also because our culture frowned on hard liquor. Eddie was selling raffle tickets to benefit the Fairbury Airport expansion at a dollar each. I bought two. Winners were to be drawn on the 4th.

July 4, 1946 started off like many other days. It was warm, but for once it was not hot and windy. I have few memories of that day except that about 5 o'clock, as I was in the barn preparing for the inevitable milking of the cows, my mother called to say I had a telephone call. I ran to the house because I received few calls and did not want to miss a one. There were the usual hellos, and then the dramatic words from the other end: "This is Fairbury (Airport) calling, Congratulations, you have just won a new 1946 Aeronca Champion airplane."

My heart skipped a few beats. I had not counted on winning. I still have that ticket, #816B. I had my choice of $2,000 or the airplane with free flight instruction. I was twenty-one years old, and I took the airplane.

The Aeronca Champion was a two-seater with a 40-foot wing span. The registration number was NC84416. It was made of tubular steel, and the fuselage and wings were covered with fabric and painted with multi-layers of acetone. Empty, it weighed 680 pounds—a big reason it was unsafe in high winds. It was really a motorized kite without a string. It carried enough fuel for four hours of flying, which meant you could go from 200 to 250 miles before refueling. It had a cruising air speed of 65 miles per hour and landed at 40. The instrument panel included an altimeter, a compass, a wind speed indicator, a gas gauge, and an rpm indicator. There was no turn and bank indicator, no radio, and, of course, none of the modern navigational devices mandatory on today's small planes.

My mother and sister Margaret were out in the farmyard. I remember racing out, taking great leaping bounds to tell them the news, yelling all the time. I had never won anything—even small.

There were other words that I cannot recall, except that I had a choice—$2,000 or the airplane, valued at about $2,500.

My dad came later, and when he heard the news he was about as excited as I. I remember asking him what I should do—take the money or the plane? To his credit he refused to tell me, but I could tell he was excited. I think he wanted me to take the plane instead of the $2,000, so I did. He was always interested in new ideas and new tools.

More surprises and decisions followed. I would need insurance. I would need a place to shelter the plane, given Nebraska's propensity to cloud up with huge storms, wind, and hail. My dad offered to build a hangar near our alfalfa field. It cost about half as much as the airplane was worth! We certified the field as an airstrip.

With the Aeronca came free flying lessons. In two weeks, I was pronounced ready to solo. It was scary. Having an airplane hangered on our farm and little money to keep it going meant I needed to make some decisions.

It took about two months to build up enough hours for my private pilot license. I had to practice figure eights, shoot landings and takeoffs, and take cross country trips.

Most of my flying was recreational. Sometimes I would take someone to a neighboring city or pick up a spare part for someone's threshing machine when that part was not available locally. Once I flew to Omaha to pick up a crankshaft. It was scary going into this big airport without a radio. All we had was a system of red and green blinking lights to signal when it was appropriate to land. I worried that I wouldn't see the lights and fly into some larger plane's path. I didn't, but it taught me the value of having a radio.

My biggest thrills came in flying my family and friends. My mother had never been on a plane until I took her up one March day. It was typically March in Nebraska with a light northwest wind and clouds at 3,500 feet. There were enough openings in the clouds, so I could get above them. She was mesmerized by the sheer whiteness of the clouds and the blueness of the sky above. I still love to be looking out the window as a plane breaks through the clouds to the pristine beauty of sunlight on clouds.

After qualifying for my private pilot license, I made the first of a number of life-changing decisions.

NORM'S LIFE LESSON #11

LUCK IS WHERE PREPARATION MEETS OPPORTUNITY.

AIRCRAFT AND ENGINE SCHOOL

Norm: My brother-in-law, Roy W. Bud Haney, and I decided that we should try to organize a flight school. I had the plane, he had the commercial and instructor's license, and 3,500 hours of combat flying as an artillery observer in the European theater. All we needed was a licensed A&E (Aircraft and Engine) mechanic, so I entered Lincoln

Aviation Institute for a year of schooling. The GI Bill covered not just flying, but mechanics school as well.

Bud was a simply superb pilot. I learned the finer points of acrobatic flying from him, doing barrel rolls and loop the loops. Once coming home, I put the Aeronica into a spin, so I could get down faster. It fell about 400 feet for each turn. But on another trip, I forgot to reset the altimeter before I left Lincoln, which was about 400 feet lower in altitude than Deshler. As I spun in to land, I realized the ground was coming up faster than it should, and I pulled out—then I found out what had happened. I was lucky. I didn't stop spinning, but I did always ask myself about that altimeter setting. While seemingly not practical, knowledge and skill at acrobatics taught one a great deal about the flight characteristics of each airplane and gave a more natural feel for what to do in an emergency.

At this time, it became more and more obvious that the future of flying was not as rosy down the road as in those early post-war years. Bud went back into the military, and I continued with aviation training, then took a job servicing planes at the Flying Service at the Hebron airport. They used my airplane for flying lessons. I lived at home and drove eight miles to work, unless I had flown home. The airport was a busy and contented place. This was a time of work and play, only the play was more.

For nearly two years, I flew that plane and enjoyed the freedom and excitement of something new. My social life was a whirl of parties and activities involving mostly my old classmates and a group of girls from Hebron. It was fun.

When I won the airplane, it was not difficult to change my career path. This abrupt change in my life was as pivotal as were some of the influential people in my life. Years later, as I reflected on my career and education path, it was obvious that I had not been entirely in control of my destiny. Isn't it strange what a one-dollar ticket can do to change a man's life and circumstances?

Do I miss that old Aeronca? There are times that I do, until I remember what that 680 pounds of wood, metal, and fabric meant to my development, moving me on to and through yet another door on my path.

QUESTIONS FOR SELF-REFLECTION

- Most of us take many years to find our calling. What back roads and detours did you take on your journey? Are you on one of those roads today? Have you thought about how to get back to the main route?
- Were any doors opened to you in your early adult life? What motivated you to walk through a specific door when it opened?
- Do you regret not walking through any open doors? If so, how can you revisit those missed opportunities that, had you taken, might have put your life on a different course?

CHAPTER 4

Watering The Soul

SPIRIT-GUIDED DECISIONS
(1948–1951)

LIFE IS REAL! LIFE IS EARNEST!
AND THE GRAVE IS NOT ITS GOAL.
—HENRY WADSWORTH LONGFELLOW

THE SURREAL BLISS OF WINNING AN AIRPLANE and soaring in the skies like Lindberg must have left Norm feeling as if he'd won the lottery of life. But once he landed back on earth—literally and metaphorically—the daily grind of serving as a mechanic and leasing his plane to training pilots for lessons closed a door for stretching his mind and imagination. It didn't take long to realize his commitment to serve others was larger than the confines of the small airport in Hebron, Nebraska.

Restlessness settled in. All those seeds planted in his childhood were desperate for nourishment, and ironically, it would be his airplane that took him to where he was meant to be—though it really was the spirit moving behind the appearances.

> *Norm:* In mid-October of 1947, after three months working at the airport, I flew from Hebron to Wisconsin where my sisters Gertrude and Eileen lived. They had married brothers Rollie and Harold Collman, also from Deshler.
>
> At the same time, my dad's doctor told my mother to get him off the farm or he'd soon be dead. So Ernie retired at forty-nine and they moved to Wisconsin Rapids to be near Gert and Eileen. My father didn't have to work, living on the little income they had from renting out the farm. They were active in their church, and one day he was asked to be a sexton—the janitor that maintains everything—and he accepted.
>
> If there was something to be done, Ernie saw to it, and he knew how to do things. He did such a good job at the church that the council asked if he'd take over janitor duties for the church's 200-student parochial school, which he also accepted. Once, my cousin Bud and I were bored at the Christmas holidays and asked if we could help him at the school. He told us to clean up one classroom. We found out later he did it over again because our work wasn't up to his standards. He never told us.
>
> But back to my airplane trip story.
>
> It's all very strange. I was twenty-two and ready for the world as it appeared out my windshield. But my inner calling was about to re-emerge.
>
> As I mapped my trip from Nebraska to Wisconsin, I saw I'd fly over northeast Iowa and the town of Waverly—the new home of my high school football coach, Wilmut Fruehling. He had finished his Ph.D. work and was teaching psychology at Wartburg College. I decided to stop over. It was a stop that changed my life.

There was a small landing trip nearby where Bill met me and took me to see the college. I was not thinking of college, so I told him of my new work. When I was leaving, as we stood on the airfield, he told me I should return to college. I laughed and said, "No way, I have a new job!" After I left, I found an admissions form tucked into the pocket of the plane with a note from Coach Fruehling asking me to think it over.

My psychology professor friend must have seen more than I could, because within three months I had traded my airplane for a new 1948 bright blue Chevrolet convertible and driven the 400 miles to Waverly, Iowa. I enrolled at Wartburg College, a small, Lutheran college of liberal learning, as a second semester freshman.

It was the third piece of a puzzle being put together without my consciously knowing what was happening. First the role I played in the Luther League, then winning an airplane, and now this trip to meet up with my old coach and enter Wartburg College. Just like that. I do not know what triggered my actions. My life had taken a dramatic turn. Years later, I reflected on this trip and my travels, and I wondered what made me do what I did.

To me then, it was only a bizarre turn of events, but years later I put this experience with others and realized that the spirit had been leading me. My prayers for a life of service had been answered, were continuing to be answered, and events were unfolding with little conscious thought or effort on my part. God had something else in mind for me, and the doors opened and closed as I wondered about my life's work.

WARTBURG COLLEGE: A HOLE WAITING TO BE FILLED

Norm's childhood experience of being a "hole waiting to be filled," a sponge eager to soak up knowledge, found pay dirt at

Wartburg. At this small-town, private Lutheran college in Iowa, the massive doors of opportunity opened to a wealth of knowledge and philosophical exploration. Norm reveled as a student, taking full advantage of the opportunity to learn and test what it meant to live a life of service. His relationships with professors and friends would remain influential over his lifetime.

> *Norm:* I drove my new, bright blue Chevrolet convertible the 400 miles to Waverly, Iowa. As I look back, the trade I'd made was almost as important as winning the airplane. Few students had cars, and a new convertible was a rarity. I was a bit uncertain and somewhat introverted, and having these wheels helped me out of that rut.
>
> The college was loaded with Army veterans, many of whom were rebelling at all the old rules and regulations. They formed a little group of revisionists, known as the Progressive Party, who didn't like the way the student government was going at the college. I was invited to join, even though I had entered at mid-year. Bob Gronlund was one of the leaders, and I became the secretary. I suspect one reason I was invited is that I had a new convertible.
>
> These were not fraternity groups complaining about social life restrictions; these were men, mostly veterans, who wanted to change the system so that it would square with what they had seen as the real world. The discussions were wide-ranging, from theology and philosophy to politics (local and national), and, of course, to women.
>
> Wartburg was an ideal place for me. It was small and personal, and the professors were dedicated to the idea of a liberal arts perspective, including a vital faith dimension in the academic traditions of German Lutheran heritage. Many of the professors were clergy who had gone on to the Ph.D. level and taught from that perspective.
>
> All this was not yet a defining moment in my development. I was too busy learning and doing to make

my own statement of what I believed. I did believe, but I could not tell you just how, or how much, not even how it would affect my life and behavior. It was like putting all that learning into a corn crib and saving it for feeding use later. I did thrive there but not so much as a scholar; rather, more as a person finding himself. I read everything and studied everything.

Wartburg did not have a journalism major, so I switched to German and later to social studies but kept up my journalism by writing for the newspaper and later becoming the Sports Information writer—unpaid except for credit by the daily papers.

My sociology professor, August Baetke, also clergy, excited me about learning. From him, I learned some of the real reasons behind racism and discrimination of all kinds. He had a great ability to see the other side of social issues and present it without bias, leaving it to his students to catch on. One thing he said that stuck:

THERE IS NO IMMEDIATE SOLUTION TO THE RACE PROBLEM, BUT IN 3,400 YEARS, IT WILL BE SOLVED BECAUSE WE WILL BECOME A NATION OF LIGHT TAN PEOPLE.

—AUGUST BAETKE, NORM'S SOCIOLOGY PROFESSOR AT WARTBURG

At Wartburg, Norm learned there is no straight path to success. He changed his major three times, and while he was enrolled pre-seminary, his only "C" was ironically in religion.

When digging through my father's files, I discovered sociology papers he kept from his work under the tutelage of Professor Baetke. My father's early exposure to the teachings of the *Golden Rule* and the Good Samaritan, and his childhood observation that skin color did not always align with these teachings, germinated as Baetke's teachings broadened his perspective on equality, race, social class, and the evolving attitudes on church and family. Being introduced to Sigmund Freud, George Herbert Mead, Ellsworth Faris, John Dewey, and the works of other predominant social psychologists of the time hastened Norm's budding reputation as a "Thinking Man."

STUDENT LIFE

Norm thrived on campus where he engaged in not one but three sports while jumping into leadership positions in student governance. I remember him telling me that he was voted "Mr. Wartburg" one year and rode a horse, dressed as the Knight mascot, in the Homecoming parade.

> *Norm:* As a junior, I ran the campaign for student body president for one of my good journalism buddies, Omar Bonderud. We lost by four votes. It set me up for running the next year, and this time we won. Not knowing much, I was not able to accomplish much, but since it was largely a ceremonial position, I learned how to respond and act.
>
> Tradition required that every student body president recruit students during the next summer before their senior year. I got the college car, a 1946 Ford, and covered five states searching for students. We had a good new class.
>
> As a senior, I had not yet found my profession. I had changed my major three times. Fifty-five of the 110 graduates of the Class of 1951 went on to the seminary. Not knowing what else to do, and in spite of getting my only "C" in my religion class, I enrolled in a pre-theological curriculum. In one sense at least, I was returning to my roots: the path of service.

TEN-MINUTE DECISION

On graduation day, Norm's destined path to the seminary was disrupted when an offer pulled him into a sudden U-turn. This ten-minute decision must have been unnerving for his parents who expected to have a minister in the family.

> *Norm:* I graduated in June of 1951 and was pre-enrolled at Wartburg Seminary for the fall of '51. Three weeks prior to graduation, the college's business manager called me in and asked me if I would be interested in taking on the job as director of admissions and public relations. I thought about it for about ten minutes and decided I did not have the call to the ministry. I accepted with no second thoughts. I had graduated by noon on June 2, said goodbye to my family, and was in my new office preparing for work at 2 p.m.
>
> My trajectory had changed once again. The calling for me to join the ministry had been very faint. The idea of parish ministry dissolved into a ministry of service to education. I believe the spirit led me to this spot for this work.

In ten minutes, my father found his "place to stand," shifting completely and immediately from being a student to becoming a sage. Preparing and unlocking young minds to lead in the future became his new job, one that was true to his calling.

BE THAT SELF WHICH ONE TRULY IS.

—SOREN KIERKEGAARD

THE THINKING MAN—MORAL LEADERSHIP AND LIFE CALLING

In the rusty old file cabinet of Norm's writings, I discovered long-buried writings revealing a prolific thinker and author of ideas as relevant today as they were seventy years ago. These themes of his lifetime are woven throughout the rest of this book, and are the foundation of his nine-month remission message to us all. As fitting with his deeply humble nature, he had tucked away these eloquent, inspiring words where they wouldn't be uncovered until our deep and prophetic discussions during his final year of life.

An introduction to his early writings begins with two summaries of pieces he wrote during his years at Wartburg: "To Thine Own Self Be True" and "On the Banks of the Cedar." The messages are the essence of his life.

TO THINE OWN SELF BE TRUE

Experience and history have proven that the moral stature of the average citizen determines the moral stature of the whole. A chain is no stronger than its weakest link. If the reformation of our world does not begin in the life of the individual, there can be no real hope for peace and contentment.

The challenge is to lose yourself in service to others so that we may all find ourselves. Paradoxical, isn't it? We are not judged so much by what we are, but by what we do with ourselves.

The great writer Shakespeare knew this when he had Hamlet say, "This, above all—To thine own self be true."

We need to be service-minded citizens for our own and others' happiness, but if this is all, then what is the larger purpose? What about the happiness of nations, of hemispheres, of the world? Should we not do something about this, too?

I found the second writing among four handwritten documents I came to refer to as his "God Is in Him" writings, all personal conversations my father had with God. One of these, "On the Banks of the Cedar," explores loneliness and introduces his lifelong dedication to the guardianship of the earth. The symbiotic relationship between weather and a bountiful harvest began on the farm, and became a metaphor for his life. After reading his words, I began to see the beacon of light residing within him, not so gently guiding him along a path where he would lead his most effective life.

ON THE BANKS OF THE CEDAR

One cool and moonlit November night, I took a lonely walk. Down to the water's edge through the rustling leaves, rudely breaking the stillness of awesome night.

Lonely but not for long, for God came too, and I walked and talked with God.

My soul cried out, But God, I'm lonely.

Look around, *said He.* What do you see?

The earth, the trees, the water, the leaves. I looked around no more than there, the beauty of nature the glory of these. The mirror of water showing that I might see the moon in the water twice pictured for me. The stars, the shadow of trees, the clouds, the smoke from a lonely flue. Showing not once but twice mirrored in blue. Who is this God who makes this true?

Shadow upon shadow joined hand in hand giving unity to nature, and in a bond lauding the glory and might of the hand which carpeted earth, which led me to walking on the cool green banks, which lived on the bay. For in the distance a lovely duck calls, hailing the night a tribute to God. Bringing the night cools, the blood grows chill, but my heart grows warmer, so does my will, as I vow to my God to serve him anew in his kingdom of glory known to so few, for it grows right beside them not alone in a pew.

Lonely I came but not lonely I left, my heart filled with love, my heart filled with God. I wonder alone, just me and my God.

I THINK THAT I SHALL NEVER SEE
A POEM AS LOVELY AS A TREE...
POEMS ARE MADE BY FOOLS LIKE ME,
BUT ONLY GOD CAN MAKE A TREE.
—JOYCE KILMER

QUESTIONS FOR SELF-REFLECTION

- Have you ever wondered if your life is unfolding according to some divine plan, and all you have to do is step through an open door? Write about such moments when you felt as if everything was flowing, you were in the zone, and you knew from an inner calling what you were supposed to do with your life.
- If you feel an inner calling different from how you are living at this moment, what is holding you back from following it? How can you move closer to it?

CHAPTER 5

Roots Take Hold

A LIFE OF SERVICE AND PARTNERSHIP (1951–1958)

BEING DEEPLY LOVED BY SOMEONE GIVES YOU STRENGTH, WHILE LOVING SOMEONE DEEPLY GIVES YOU COURAGE.

—LAO TZU

I TRY TO IMAGINE HOW NORM'S PARENTS Nora and Ernie must have reacted, driving back on the four-hour road to home after their son—their only child to graduate from college—had told them minutes after the ceremony that he was withdrawing from the seminary to go to work for Wartburg College. They wouldn't have even arrived home before he entered his new office and gotten busy that day. How I wish a mobile phone video could have captured that moment!

Norm had found his "place to stand" and jumped feet first into the world of higher education, an ideal environment, it would turn out, for his mission of shaping young minds. Grounded in deeply embedded values from childhood, he packed those values up and took them to work.

Outside of the college bubble, our country experienced rapid-pace change and innovation that most certainly caught Norm's attention. It was the '50s. Color TV came into our living rooms. The U.S. Air Force had flown the Lucky Lady II nonstop around the world in ninety-four hours and one minute at the same time when war was brewing in Korea. Brown vs. the Board of Education ended segregation (though there were unfortunate outcomes for formerly segregated teachers and students). Senator Joseph McCarthy testified on alleged communist interference into the U.S. military, eerily foreshadowing real-life events of today.

Popular culture was changing, and it was changing fast. Our waistlines expanded when McDonald's franchised fast food, and wallets opened wide when Walt Disney invited families to Disneyland. I'm sure Norm was following closely when Rosa Parks, a seamstress on her way home from work, refused to give up her seat on a bus to a white man, leading to segregation on buses being declared unconstitutional.

Fueled with eternal optimism and a measure of idealism, Norm's thoughts turned to work and finding a life partner. Meeting Jeanette "Jo" Kosbau led to a perfect match of soulmates.

SERVANT LIFE AT WORK

When your vocation meshes with personal values, passion is ignited, and work becomes a joyful experience. A full-steam work ethic, striving for excellence, and the opportunity to shape fertile minds occupied Norm's every moment—until he caught sight of Jo, the woman who became my mom.

Norm tells about his life at work:

> *Norm:* Accepting the job as director of admission and public relations at Wartburg College was a clear statement

saying I wanted to serve this college for what it did for me and for what it does for young people, in terms of the Lutheran sense of having a calling.

Wartburg was accredited the year I arrived. It was small, ill-endowed with inadequate facilities, and located in a small Iowa town, but there were those who loved her, and I was one of them.

I was busy because in addition to admissions and public relations, I was also in charge of alumni activity, publicity, publications, campus events, and concert promotion. I also booked the choir and band tours. My salary was meager $285 per month. My work hours were often 8 a.m. to 10 p.m. I loved my work and my college.

NORM'S LIFE LESSON #12

ONCE YOU WALK THROUGH AN OPEN DOOR TO YOUR FUTURE, DO YOUR BEST WORK. GIVE IT YOUR ALL. "MEASURE TWICE, SAW ONCE."

The first task was to recruit the fall class of new students. What I did not understand very well about this sudden job opportunity was that Wartburg was retrenching in anticipation of a drop-in enrollment. There was now a dwindling supply of veterans, multitudes of whom had jammed the college earlier. Years later, I realized that the college had taken a major gamble by hiring a neophyte in a job that could make or break the budget for the coming year. Blissfully ignorant, I did not understand that I was set up for possible failure.

I drove about 50,000 miles that summer, experiencing the heartland states—Iowa, Illinois, Indiana, Wisconsin, Minnesota, North and South Dakota, Kansas, Missouri, and Colorado. I visited 700 pastors, many of whom were hungry for outside contact. I was like the Internet, connecting widely and bringing the world in. In return, pastors shared their confirmation lists of potential students for Wartburg.

The first year, we brought in two more students than the previous year. We were the only college in Iowa to go up in enrollment—all because I did not know I was supposed to fail. It was later that demographic studies showed I had unwittingly embarked on a major recruiting effort before other colleges were doing it. I had stumbled into the vanguard of the nation's unprecedented growth in the number of high school graduates going to college.

Change was already at hand, but it took several years for me to begin what later became a way of life—looking ahead!

NORM'S LIFE LESSON #13

YOU CAN WORK MIRACLES WHEN YOU DON'T KNOW THAT SOMETHING IS IMPOSSIBLE.

Ever cognizant of the injustice of inequality, Norm instinctively employed a grassroots strategy, that of changing one life at a time. It was a concept he incorporated throughout his lifetime, at work and at home. It was an instinct I inherited, or perhaps I learned it by observation. No matter, it would become the foundation for my own calling, namely my global work with Dining for Women: change the world one person at a time. And as I've found over the past fifteen years, it works even on a global scale. Norm tells of his efforts:

Norm: In admissions, I first encountered international black students and worked to get them in. After graduating, one

I'd recruited returned home to Nigeria and became that country's attorney general. Another was a doctor who went back home and started a school for kids. At vacation times, they couldn't go home and couldn't stay on campus because it closed, so we'd have them over for meals. I taught them how to do dishes, and many were amazed a male would do things like that. It changed them. It changed us. They learned something about cultural differences in America that they didn't see in Tanzania.

Tanzania... This thread of international exchange is woven throughout his life, emerging in a colorful fabric during the years of his retirement. Norm would have unfinished business with the people of Tanzania.

Before we move on to how he met and married Jo, here is an excerpt from Norm's first address to students, demonstrating his approach to shaping the minds of the students—intellectually and morally. Note the emergence of three key questions, another theme that would play out over his lifetime of service, both personally and when his time came to train others in leadership and management.

WARTBURG COLLEGE FIRST ADDRESS: YOUR MISSION IN LIFE

Have you ever wondered, What am I going to do with my life? *Am I heading in the right direction? Am I making the most of my talents? What are my talents?*

It's easy to lose your mission in life in the maze of possibilities. It may be helpful to remember the wisdom found in Matthew 6:34: Therefore, do not be anxious about tomorrow, for tomorrow will be anxious for itself. Let the day's own trouble be sufficient for the day.

Let's explore how you might find the answer by asking yourself three very important questions.

What are you? *You are a living creature on God's good earth, bound to its laws and restrictions and its blessings.*

Who are you? *You are a child of God, created with body, soul, and spirit. You have the freedom to choose between good or evil. And God watches over you and urges you to do the right things.*

What are you going to do about it? *Submit, body and soul, with prayer and humility. God is guiding you, leading you into ways you don't know and can't recognize until you are there.*

What does all this have to do with your life and your life mission?

It means that you are on earth with a certain amount of freedom to do as you please, and you receive blessings with which to work for good in this world.

It means, as Phillip says in Galatians 6:7: A man's harvest in life will depend entirely on what he sows. *It means that you should choose your life's work according to your talents and capabilities, and whatever you do, do it with zeal and fire, as if there were no tomorrow, so when the flame is sniffed out, there may be no waste left behind.*

NORM'S LIFE LESSON #14

SEARCH FOR TRUTH. NEVER STOP LEARNING.

A "MEANT TO BE" MARRIAGE

Norm's success in admissions further fueled his work, though his story is interrupted by what he called "the most important event in my entire life"—meeting my mother, Jo Kosbau. Theirs was a true love match, a rare equal partnership and an example for the strength that comes to an individual because of the selection of a mate.

In a second "God Is In Him" writing (where he seems to be speaking directly to God), he again wrestles with loneliness, and questions whether his commitment to a servant life leaves room for love and marriage.

WHAT IF THE LORD HAS NEED OF ME?

I don't get it. I left her but two hours ago. Now I'm empty. Part of me stayed with her and I'm lonely, my heart cries out of emptiness. It must be loneliness, it can't be love—love isn't like that, love is supposed to be exciting and romantic, and I 'm content just to see her, look at her, listen to her, feel her near me.

Maybe—and I've often wondered—God is calling me, and either I can't or won't understand what to do. Maybe the spirit is wrestling with me, and a higher calling awaits me. Maybe I'm exaggerating my own importance. I pray, Lord, if thou wouldst have me to be a better servant, send her to me or me to her. Help me to find the part of me that is missing and keeps my soul wandering restlessly.

I cannot think with my heart, and my heart tells me I'm in love. I can't stop. It's like an addiction, I can't get away. Morning noon and night, it's there—which way can I turn? I stop to catch my breath, and it is breathed into me—despair, joy, satisfaction, anxiety, jubilance, contentment, all rolled up into me.

I give up. I surrender to love.

In the early 1950s, it wasn't proper to directly ask a woman on a date without an introduction. My father once told me he watched Jo in town, recalling her red, fitted, long winter coat with fur trim. When they did finally go on a blind date, she wasn't as enamored as he, but she saw depth, freedom, and openness. He saw a career woman, beauty, intelligence, openness to life, and love for all, especially those in most need, the underdog. Unusual for the time, both Norm and Jo had established careers before meeting and marrying at age twenty-eight.

Norm: Life became at once more complicated and meaningful when I met Jo. I had seen her many times at Roy's Diner or at Dillavou's. We were formally introduced at a night of bridge playing at the home of my boss and his wife who happened to be a a teacher at the school where Jo taught in Waverly. The match-making worked, but Jo's version of that first encounter showed me later that she was considerably less impressed with me than I with her.

We met and were married within six months, on June 30, 1953. We were twenty-eight. It was a "meant to be" merger. My family loved her. Her family was not quite that sure about me, but I did not have time to think about it. I assumed that was what everyone did and that we had to learn how to live together.

NORM'S LIFE LESSON #15

IT'S AN OPPORTUNITY CORNER.

(WHEN LUCK OR GOOD CIRCUMSTANCES CAME KNOCKING, AS WELL AS A REFERENCE TO DRIVING WITH YOUR DATE AND TAKING ADVANTAGE OF A CURVE IN THE ROAD TO SIT CLOSER TOGETHER)

AN INTERVIEW WITH MY PARENTS: A "MEANT TO BE" MARRIAGE

NORM'S VERSION OF THEIR COURTSHIP

Norm: She's one of a million. I've never said this but talk about the door opening. I always saw her in town. Dressed to the nines. A gorgeous fourth grade teacher, and when she arrived at class in the morning, everyone knew she was there. Beautiful, black hair. Piercing eyes.

Barb: How did she behave toward you when you first met her?

Norm: She was alright. She didn't come over and make me feel I was being overrun. I had to do a little achieving on my own. I didn't know what I was doing. Amazing.

Barb: You met, and did you ask her out?

Norm: This was in July and she didn't return to Waverly until school began again in September. That was my busiest travel time in admissions. Our first date was in October at Homecoming. By Christmas, we were engaged. Married the next June.

JO'S VERSION OF THEIR COURTSHIP

Barb: You met him, and it was pretty quick then?

Jo: We were close to twenty-nine. A co-teacher, Verna, wanted me to meet this eligible bachelor who had a Studebaker.

Barb: What was your first impression?

Jo: It wasn't a lightning bolt. I thought he was an intellectual snob—quoting Shakespeare, the Bible.

Barb: So why him?

Jo: We had the same values but different upbringings. Norwegian Lutherans were strict. When I found out that I could dance, drink and play cards, and still get to heaven, I decided a German Lutheran man was preferable to a Norwegian.

Barb: You were the spark to his quiet nature. He loved your rebellious, open spirit.

Jo: There wasn't any pushing or pulling. We were going in the same direction, and that's rare.

ABOUT JO

To understand my parents' highly successful and unique marriage, there are a few things to know about what shaped Jo. Her early environment was restrictive and at times tragic. It forbade alcohol, dance, and even a friendly game of cards. Emotions were tamped down, and freedom tightly controlled. Not once does she remember hearing the words *I love you* spoken by her own mother. My mother never shared much about her upbringing, so I was riveted hearing her story unfold in our conversations with my father, and later after his passing when she lived with me.

> *Norm:* Jo's family settled into farming in northeast Iowa around the end of the Civil War. They were Norwegian-German Lutherans, dominated more by the Norwegian side of her mother, Alma, than her father, Charles Kosbau. When the Depression hit, her family lost their farm, and Alma began teaching in a one-room country school, earning $30 per month to support the six children at home.

Jo's mother never really smiled or showed affection. It may have been triggered when Alma's own parents distanced themselves from her when she married Charles Kosbau, believing she married beneath her class. Alma's father was the town assessor and had a big office downtown, eating lunch off white linen tablecloths. When she married a farm boy, she was cut off from the family, and never inherited any of the family's wealth.

One day in fifth grade, Jo's whole life was disrupted when she opened the front door to get the paper and saw the headlines. There it was for all to see: her father was in jail. The Depression had led him to take desperate measures, and his theft of pigs for food had landed him in prison. Jo's stoic Norwegian mother made sure no one *ever* talked about Jo's father's sentence (Jo's sister Ruth carried it to her grave at ninety-nine), even as her three brothers at home were sent off in the middle of the night to live with neighbors because she could no longer afford to feed them. Since my mother had a loving relationship with her father, I can only imagine her devastation. Charles eventually came home but wouldn't find work in their small town of Waukon until a few years later.

Alma walked miles to teach in a one-room country school, and somehow put all six children through college, four of them including my mother becoming educators. She was too proud to accept help, even the government program for free butter and milk. Pride of independence ran large in this generation of ancestors.

Jo graduated from high school in 1942 and went to the University of Iowa, where her brothers and sisters had gone. In the first semester of college, Jo found herself in a pool, when learning to swim was a requirement of the nursing school. Being deathly afraid of water, she dropped out, packed her suitcase, called her mom, and boarded a greyhound bus for home, intending to work at the local five-and-dime. But her mother met her at the bus depot and put her on a two o'clock bus heading to Luther College where Jo would go on to earn a teaching degree.

Jo was a feminist before there were feminists. Unmarried and a career woman at age twenty-eight, she taught fourth grade in Waverly, a small town in Iowa, where her brother also taught. When she found out he was earning a lot more money than she was, simply for being male, she marched into the school board office and demanded equal pay. And she got it.

Then at 29, she made one of the best decisions of her life when she met and married my father. A man who would treat her as an equal partner for the rest of her life. Although she insisted she wasn't as starry eyed as he was, their disparate stories of their beginning became unified following a short courtship which may sound like a Hollywood love story. Like most love stories, it was not without sorrow.

> *Norm:* At age twenty-eight, we were both settled into jobs and routines, and ready for marriage. After the wedding, there was no pregnancy for almost a year, then the sorrow of losing a first born at childbirth showed us we dare not take

> anything for granted. Our first one, Mary Jo, was born two months early in 1955, and our hearts were broken when she died right after birth. I was thunderstruck. I didn't know I had emotions like that. Went home and cried all by myself. Jo was still in the hospital. Sixty some years ago.
>
> Then babies started coming in rapid succession. Peggy on August 2, 1956. Bill on July 24, 1957. Barb, thirteen months later on August 20, 1958. We became proud owners of 101 Sunset, an 840-square-foot house, purchased for $10,200. It had three small bedrooms, one just large enough for a crib, and no garage. But it was ours.

My parents named my brother Bill after social activist William Allen White, a famous Kansas journalist and author who became the iconic voice of Middle America. White's message encouraged a viable moral order through community, and he vigorously spoke out against the Ku Klux Klan. Very apropos considering my father's calling in life.

The complexity and emotional wasteland of my mom's childhood layered a deep understanding and empathy for people. She became a healer of lost souls and champion of the underdog. She loved people deeply. She gave out all the energy and love that was withheld from her as a child. She expressed herself, and let you know exactly what she thought, like it or not.

Her natural charisma was a magnet for drawing people near to her. Norm's eyes always lit up when she walked into the room. He only had eyes for Jo.

EQUALITY: A RIGHT

> *Norm:* I call ours an "equal partner" marriage. It is hard for me to imagine what my life (or hers) would have been like without the merging of our two streams into a river for a new family. This dual influence on our work and offspring came from the deep-seated values of our Norwegian and German Lutheran heritage.

> My prize is my partner who shared my life for sixty-four years. She has the easiest, most enlightened grasp of where someone else is. She looks into their eyes and somehow senses it, even though she herself doesn't really know. But she knows how to comfort. Amazing.
>
> Why do people love her? She is like an open invitation to talk about what might trouble you. She can see your soul when she looks in your eyes. She gives people permission to unload, and they are loyal to her for life.

Both my parents believed that education shapes your life, and that equality is not a privilege but a basic human right. They were an effective pairing, a balance of my father's open yet quiet nature with my mother's dynamic personality that captured the hearts of everyone she knew. As their children—Peggy, Bill, and I—know, we were especially blessed to have had Norm and Jo as our parents.

NORM'S LIFE LESSON #16

FIND A PARTNER YOU RESPECT, ONE THAT LIFTS THE LEVEL OF YOUR BEHAVIOR AND LIFE GOALS, PERHAPS WITHOUT YOU EVEN KNOWING IT.

QUESTIONS FOR SELF-REFLECTION

- If money didn't matter, what would be your dream job?
- If you are unfulfilled in your work, what is holding you back from making changes? How might you take a step forward?
- What values do you share with your life partner? If you're not married, what values are important to find in a partner?
- Do you consider your relationship with your life partner an equal one? If not, what might you do differently to change that?

CHAPTER 6

Facing the Sun

AN EMERGING MESSAGE (1950s)

YOU CANNOT TEACH A MAN ANYTHING. YOU CAN ONLY HELP HIM DISCOVER IT WITHIN HIMSELF.

—GALILEO

NORM FOUND TIME TO REVEL IN INTELLECTUAL, PHILOSOPHICAL, AND SPIRITUAL THOUGHT, as he drove thousands of miles on backroads through the Midwest. My mom's first impression of him was as an intellectual snob, that his head was in the clouds. That's because it was. Oh my, how he thrived in that head space!

I found evidence of burgeoning intellect in many of his writings from that time, revealing his developing moral imperatives that were far ahead of the curve for someone in his mid-twenties to early thirties. Here we see his values, faith, and openness at play. We see the beginning of his vision for enriching young minds and moral challenges relevant for us all, even today. He was a lover of thought. His musings far outreached his years.

Norm held on to favorite books, some from nearly seventy years ago, by authors who never grew old to him. In his treasured books, he read and unearthed the foundation for the development of his leadership and managerial style, for both his personal and professional life.

I wish I would have heard him speak more about these values during my lifetime. Maybe I would have paid more attention and caught on more quickly. Maybe I would have found my calling earlier or understood how his vision planted seeds of my own. At this state of his life, his persona as *a thinking man* emerges with wisdom for us all.

LIFELONG LEARNING

With a steep learning curve in his new position and a standard of excellence, Norm began searching for resources to learn. Seeking knowledge and truth was as natural to him as a breath of fresh air. As he settled into his work at Wartburg, once again he began filling that 'hole.' this commitment to learning would last throughout his lifetime.

> *Norm:* Learning is like going into a garden and seeing new plants never seen before. Gorgeous. Open them up and enjoy them; smell the fragrance of new ideas or old ideas reborn.
>
> In the 1950s, I dug myself into society through reading and educating myself, and engaging in the community by joining organizations, including the Chamber of Commerce, the Lions Club, and the Young Republicans Council. I guess I always threw myself into whatever I was doing. I mean, I took something when I did it and didn't look back. If we knew how that worked, we'd design a

pattern and make cookie cutters, but we don't know. I just knew I had to keep bettering myself.

Early on, I realized how precious little I knew about my field. For years, I collected "think pieces" as they were available to me and read all the publications I could find. I subscribed to advertising services. A number of publications came to me as the public relations director, or maybe because no one else wanted them: *The American College Public Relations Association, The Public Relations Association, The Public Relations Society of America,* IBM's *Think* magazine, *The Kaiser Alumni News.* It was in these pages that I first met the great educator and statesman John W. Gardner. I was exposed to theories of motivation put to work in the world of business. These influences grabbed my thinking processes and stimulated them in ways I had never imagined possible.

A BEACON OF VALUES

Throughout his career, Norm was asked to speak on topics of education, leadership, morality, equality, and service to one another. Dating back to his Wartburg years, he began exploring and honing his messages, where he would challenge his audiences on values. For him, living your most effective life began with defining your internal belief system and from there finding your place to stand.

NORM'S LIFE LESSON #17

THE BEST SERMONS ARE LIVED, NOT PRESENTED.

I've selected five writings to summarize, from the 1950s, that touch upon values Norm lived every day and are expressions of the life lessons he was learning and sharing. The first is a speech, "The Sword of Decency," given after joining Toastmasters, a group he joined when he realized that his decision not to enter the seminary meant he needed another avenue for learning how to be persuasive in his oratory skills. He called on people to do what is right and live a life of service.

THE SWORD OF DECENCY

We Americans have developed what I call a social conscience—a respect for the rights of others—and a knowledge that democracy must be guarded at all times by alert, thinking citizens like you and me.

The challenge today is to pick up the sword of decency and determination to fight for the good and noble things of life. To strike out in a venture aimed at harmonizing the world.

This new venture is a life of service. We are judged not so much by what we are, but by what we do with ourselves.

The second writing, "Citizens of Heaven" was written in the 1950s for an unknown audience. He urges people to think beyond their backyards and spread morality through our youth. Norm's early instinctual strategy for change was to build a movement, changing one life at a time.

CITIZENS OF HEAVEN—GLOBAL VISION

As citizens of heaven, we need to be involved with the world. It is the responsibility of the congregation and its pastor to prepare its youth to be citizens of heaven—both the college-bound and the job-bound. They need preparation for living and for personal involvement in the life of the world. We need to mobilize ourselves to reach out one-by-one, two-by-two, or by the thousands.

In a third writing, "Letting Go of Fear to Find Peace," Norm shares the story of Roland Hays who demonstrated the power of peace in fighting the battle of inequality.

LETTING GO OF FEAR TO FIND PEACE—EQUALITY AND PEACE

Roland Hays, the famed Black American tenor of a generation ago, was scheduled to sing in Berlin in 1924 at a time when feelings ran high against the African American troops of the French occupation of the Rhine. So high in fact, that the American consul received letters protesting the performance, with the implication that an African American should not insult the spirit of great German writers by singing plantation songs in Beethoven Hall.

Hays tells this story:

"The hall was packed with people, with hundreds standing. At 8 o'clock, I walked onto the stage, greeted by a barrage of hisses full of hatred.

"I had never experienced this before. But I remembered my mission. I did then what I have always done at the beginning of a concert. When I step on any stage I recall that I am merely an instrument through which my mission is being fulfilled.

"I stood there with hands clasped, praying that I might be entirely blotted out of the picture: that the people sitting there might feel only the spirit of God flowing through melody and rhythm; that racial and national prejudices might be forgotten.

"Usually when I do that sincerely, the audience instinctively feels what is happening as I commune with God. But this was the hardest audience I ever faced. Two minutes, three, four, five, on into an interminable ten minutes, the hissing continued. Then the hissing and stamping of feet suddenly stopped.

"I asked my accompanist to take out the sheet music for Schubert's Thou Art My Peace. *As the clear notes of the song floated out over the crowd, a silence fell on them.*

"It was not a personal victory. It was the victory of a power which is far greater than I am, a power strong enough to subdue the hatred in that Berlin audience."

My father summarizes the lesson from his story:

> *Norm:* God brought peace to that hostile audience through a peace which comes from within, for all the outer influences were born of hatred and jealousy. Somehow the spirit subdued the savage hearts of his listeners, and the *Peace of God which passeth all understanding* came upon them.
>
> What I learned from this is that bravery and courage come from letting go of fear. I am reminded that I am but a small speck on the planet and not in control of my life as much as I might think I am.

A fourth writing from this time, "The *Golden Rule*," exemplifies an overarching value that defined Norm wherever he went. Like the kindness embodied by his mother, this message of treating others as you would want to be treated yourself crosses over multiple religions, and Norm spent his lifetime nurturing others in this spirit of love.

THE GOLDEN RULE—*KINDNESS AND LOVE*

> *Matthew 7:12: "Thou shalt love thy neighbor as thyself."*
>
> *It would be a different world if we would really try this rule of kindness instead of letting selfishness rule us.*
>
> *Think about what you did today.* Did I argue with a friend and roommate? Envy someone else's clothes, books, or ball? Have I been unkind to anyone?
>
> *If you haven't followed the rule of kindness, why not? Is it because you don't take the words seriously? Is it because it is easy to think someone is not your neighbor? Your neighbor is anyone on this whole earth who needs you, needs your help. It matters not whether their face is black, yellow, brown, or white, whether they are Russian, Arab, or Jewish. If they need your help, they are your neighbors.*
>
> *The next time you're going somewhere with Johnny, and he is late, don't think,* He's late, I'll go on without him. It will serve him right. *Wait! Suppose you were the one who*

was late, wouldn't you be glad if Johnny waited for you? Or suppose that Mary has trouble with her studies and needs help. Do you think, Oh, let her get it by herself—I did. *Stop and think of how much you would appreciate a kindly bit of assistance.*

Start your life of kindness with the little things, because after all, it is these little things which, knowingly or not, we appreciate most deeply. Try kindness on the person who sleeps next to you, on a study partner, at dinner, and in the classroom. Know what it means to live by the Golden Rule: *To do unto others as you would have them do unto you. It will make you honest, kind, and good. The way we ought to be.*

Something I revered most about my father was his ability to remain judgment free of other people. He saw both sides and never, ever spoke negatively about anyone. He looked for and found the best in people. This is the one quality of his that I try to emulate every day. I do not always succeed. But I try.

GRANT THAT I MAY NOT CRITICIZE MY NEIGHBOR
UNTIL I HAVE WALKED A MILE IN HIS MOCCASINS.
—AMERICAN INDIAN PRAYER

In this fifth writing, "Don't Tear Him Down, Build Him Up," he zeroes in on judgment.

DON'T TEAR HIM DOWN, BUILD HIM UP

Webster defines a critic *as "one who expresses a reasoned opinion on any matter involving a judgment of its value, truth, or righteousness, or an appreciation of its beauty or technique."*

Negative criticism I would define as unreasoned opinion, stemming not so much from accurate judgment as from the emotions of fear, envy, and malice.

Don't tear him down, build him up.

If a classmate gets an A, don't grouse about the professor, favoritism, and luck. Congratulate them and say, If I work harder the next six weeks, maybe I can earn one, too.

If that girl down the hall is elected Fall Queen, let her know you are thrilled. You know we can enjoy such things vicariously, just as easily as we can suffer vicariously.

I don't mean you should scrap criticism, not at all, but let's scrap what I call negative criticism—that which leads not toward greater achievement but to the scrap heap.

NORM'S LIFE LESSON #18

IF YOU DON'T HAVE ANYTHING GOOD TO SAY, DON'T SAY ANYTHING. ALWAYS TAKE THE HIGH ROAD.

I Googled this phrase—*take the high road*—and learned it was popularized in 1948 as part of negative campaigning tactics between presidential candidates Thomas Dewey and Harry Truman. After seventy years, too many in our country are stuck in the mud of the low road. We need Norm's example to spread and take hold, inspiring more of our leaders to take the high road.

OPENING THE MIND—INFLUENCERS

Norm searched for the truth all his life. There's a trail of his search throughout his writings, and in one of our final conversations he spoke about seeking truth. I remember the intensity of his blue eyes when he told me, "I don't know it all." It's an admission I wished I'd explored more thoroughly and one he related to leading morally. He said this during a discussion of the current world and national leadership situation.

What is the truth? Googling pops up many different kinds—scientific, historical, intellectual, logical, spiritual, moral. How do we define it? Moral truth begs the question: who sets the standard? Thus, my own search for the source of truth began.

My quest to understand took me to my father's treasured books and quote collection on philosophy, theology, leadership, business, and management. From his underlined passages and bookmarked pages, he gravitated to big, curious questions. Truth, innovation, change, and his passion, moral leadership. Four key influencers shaped Norm's life and work.

THE TRUTH WILL SET YOU FREE.
—JOHN 8:32

SÖREN KIERKEGAARD—TRUTH, JUDGMENT, INDIVIDUALITY

Danish philosopher Sören Kierkegaard, a Christian existential thinker in the mid-nineteenth century, pondered issues such as individualism, morality, and faith. Kierkegaard introduced Norm to the individual's continual process of becoming, of searching for the truth. Interestingly, in *Purity of Heart Is To Will One Thing* (1938), my father underlined "noetic," meaning related to mental activity or the intellect.

Kierkegaard defined objective truths as final and static, and subjective truth as continuing and dynamic. He objected to objective truth as the way to know life or the truth of existence. He claimed that a human cannot find truth separate from the subjective experience of one's own existing, defined by the values and fundamental essence that consist of one's way of life.

In the same book, Norm paid close attention to two passages, the first on judgment, and the second on individuality and thinking for oneself:

"If you judge, you must bear the responsibility for your judgment. It will teach you that you should examine what you understand and what you do not understand, as if you stood trembling in the presence of a departed one.

For many fools do not make a wise man, and the crowd is a doubtful recommendation for a cause. The larger the crowd, the more probably that that which it praises is folly..."

THE MOST COMMON FORM OF DESPAIR IS NOT BEING WHO YOU ARE... LIFE HAS ITS OWN HIDDEN FORCES WHICH YOU CAN ONLY DISCOVER BY LIVING. —SÖREN KIERKEGAARD

DANIEL BURNHAM—THINK BIG, EMBRACE CHANGE

A second influencer, Daniel Burnham, a Chicago architect and city planner, believed there was, in my father's words, "no room for timid plans." This idea was a green light to Norm, freeing him to look into the future and dream big. Nothing is impossible. These words carried Norm over five decades, resurfacing long after he retired and his passion to serve took him to Tanzania.

In Burnham's words (as quoted in *Daniel H. Burnham, Architect, Planner of Cities* by Charles Moore, 1921):

"Make no little plans. They have no magic to stir men's blood and probably will not be realized. Make big plans: aim high in hope and work... long after we are gone will be a living thing asserting itself with ever-growing insistence. Let your watchword be order and your beacon beauty. Think big!"

JOHN W. GARDNER—NURTURING HUMAN POTENTIAL AND ADOPTING CHANGE

A third influencer, John Gardner, validated what Norm learned from his own father, that adopting change needs to be a way of life. That change is a resource in developing human and organizational potential, or as Gardner surmised, personal and societal change is inevitable and a necessary source of renewal.

In the 1950s, when Gardner was president of Carnegie Corporation and head of the Carnegie Foundation for the Advancement of Teaching, he gave a speech entitled, "The Ever-Renewing Society." Norm saved a copy, and the underlined passages, quoted below, reveal an uncanny parallel between the vocations and philosophies of both men. I see where Norm developed a strong distaste for the status quo.

"When we talk about revitalizing a society… the problem is breaking through the crusty rigidity and stubborn complacency of the status quo.

The development of resistance to new ideas is a familiar process in the individual. The infant is a model of openness to new experience—receptive, curious, eager, unafraid, willing to try anything. As the years pass these priceless qualities fade. One becomes more cautious, less eager, and accumulates deeply rooted habits and fixed attitudes.

'Creativity' is a kind of psychic wonder drug, powerful and presumably painless; and everyone wants a prescription.

The ever-renewing society will be a free society. It will understand that the only stability possible today is stability in motion… Free society must foster a climate in which the seedlings of new ideas can survive, and the deadwood of ideas be hacked out."

HERMANN HESSE—PREPARING THE NEXT GENERATION FOR CHANGE

A fourth influencer was Hermann Hesse, a German author and existentialist who challenged Norm's thoughts and shaped his belief in the importance not only of change, but of preparing the next generation to embrace change. In a speech Norm gave to educational and church leaders, entitled "The Age of Overlap," he cited Hesse's words from his novel *Steppenwolf*, to explain the problem in society between the extremes of division on the left and right or front and back:

"Every age, every culture, every custom and tradition has its own character, its own weakness, and its own strength... accepts certain sufferings as a matter of course, puts up patiently with certain evils. Human life is reduced to real suffering only when two ages, two cultures and religions overlap... Now there are times when a whole generation is caught in this way between two ages, two modes of life, with the consequence that it loses all power to understand itself...

[One's] whole life was an example that love of one's neighbors is not possible without love of oneself."

Norm went on in his speech to say:

When a whole generation loses its power to understand itself, we reach the grace point of zero, something Germans call die gnade des nullpuktes. *When things absolutely cannot get worse, when they are at the very lowest ebb, then Grace still abounds, and it becomes possible to do things no one would have thought of or permitted before. Change is with us, and we need to welcome it. We need to address it before individuals get to the hardening point, resistant to change.*

There is no room for doubt that Norm carried his values wherever he went, or that personal evolution was a way he lived and encouraged all to do. We may not all find ourselves in value-rich working environments, though such environments shouldn't put up a roadblock to effectiveness and promotion through individual development.

With all his learning and provocative thinking, I can understand how he reached a point where he was outgrowing his source of knowledge and truth in his position at Wartburg College. After many years, he reached a plateau and got an itch for an advanced degree. He knocked on the next door, and it opened to his next step.

QUESTIONS FOR SELF-REFLECTION

- What were the strongest influences on you during your early adult years?
- Do you proactively continue to learn and develop both at work and as an individual? If not, what's holding you back? Where might you start?
- What are the values of your work environment? What values do you use in your work?

PART II

The Growing Season

1958–1989

CHAPTER 7

Cultivation

ANOTHER DOOR OPENS
(1958–1960)

THERE IS NOTHING NEW UNDER THE SUN.
—ECCLESIASTES 1:9

NORM OFTEN REFERRED TO HIMSELF AS AN "ECLECTIC PRAGMATIC," one who takes wisdom from many sources and uses it to live well. His voracious search for knowledge intensified after seven years at Wartburg College, prompting him to request a sabbatical year to pursue an advanced degree. Having three children under the age of three and the prospect of a reduced income didn't slow him down. Instead of adversity, he only saw opportunity. He and Jo packed their bags and on August 30, 1958, headed west to Madison, Wisconsin.

> *Norm:* At this time in my life, while I loved my work and loved what I was doing at Wartburg College—in large part because

> I loved my alma mater—I kept looking for more, for something else. I had read all the literature in my field and went to every available conference, and still I felt the need for more training. When I discovered that Scott Cutlip, who had written most of the good textbooks on public relations, headed that department at the University of Wisconsin, another door opened for me to walk through and follow the path to where I was meant to be.

OUR BEST YEAR: GRADUATE SCHOOL HOUSING

Norm's optimism shines as he describes life in the fishbowl of married student housing at the University of Wisconsin, with kids running and crawling all around him and Jo at a time when cloth diapers were the only option.

> *Norm:* Our best year as a family was the year we spent on my sabbatical at the University of Wisconsin. It was the first time that Jo and I moved away from what was familiar and shared an adventure, all on our own.
>
> We had Peggy and Bill, and as luck would have it, our youngest, Barbara, was born nine days before we left for Madison. Our little Studebaker with a 4x7 U-Haul in tow huffed and puffed, drinking gasoline like a Buick, but we made it in comparatively good time of five and one-half hours. My mother was with us to ride herd on the kids, and she held the baby on her lap for the 200-mile trip.
>
> We arrived at Eagle Heights to our two-bedroom apartment in graduate school housing. In the twelve buildings, there were a total of twenty-six children under five! At night, all we could hear was the wind in the trees and the occasional cry from one of the children in our own or the neighboring apartments.
>
> We struggled. Laundry privileges were two hours a week, and we had three in diapers. We lived on half pay

from the College—$2,600—and a $1,600 assistantship from the university. Adversity does breed character.

We shopped for used living room furniture and bought an old sofa bed for $25—grey tweed. Then we found a used, faded brownish-tweed rocking chair, a necessity with three babies. With this drab hodge-podge of furniture, we bought bright drapes from Montgomery Ward to perk up the room: red, green, tan, pink, and black on a white background. We bought five pairs to fit our big picture window, only to find we didn't buy enough. Right before we were heading out to buy more, the mailman came with a package from Etta, Jo's sister-in-law, with some green drapes she wasn't using. We sewed them onto the outside of our others, and they looked pretty nice.

Sleep was a major problem. Peggy had colic. She would awaken between 11 and 2, crying and needing to be rocked back to sleep. That was my job. Jo needed her rest to cope with the children all day long. But to top it off, Peggy would awaken every morning between 4:30 and 5:30, so my own sleep was both interrupted and shortened. This went on for a month or so before a pediatrician prescribed a medicine that helped us all sleep more soundly.

My dad told me in his last days that when he looked back on this time, he knew it was the year he grew up and realized who he was.

NORM'S LIFE LESSON #19

HOME IS WHEREVER YOU LAY YOUR HEAD.
EVERY MOVE BROADENS YOUR MIND.

FROM JOURNALISM TO HIGHER EDUCATION

At the University of Wisconsin (UW), Norm enrolled in the School of Journalism to study under the tutelage of a renowned public relations and journalism expert, only to be immediately redirected by that expert to a different study altogether. Three key professors would further his understanding of theories related to motivation, leadership, and decision making, reinforcing his belief that being open to change and innovation is a vital component to success.

> *Norm:* I enrolled in the School of Journalism because of Professor Scott Cutlip, a foremost expert in his field. As my advisor, he helped me see that I did not really want a journalism and public relations degree, but rather that I needed to prepare myself for a career in education administration. This was not my doing. I followed.
>
> Instead of loading me with journalism courses, he advised me to take only the essential journalism courses, and then he got me enrolled with three of UW's best teachers: Ralph Huitt in political science, J. Kenneth Little in education, and Leonard Berkowizc in psychology.
>
> From Huitt, I learned it's not the politicians who hold the power but rather the highest bureaucrat who can't lose his job when there is a change in administration because he's under contract. From Little, I learned about education and leadership. From Berkowizc, I learned how the mind works and how to motivate people to get things done. I also learned about the need to set direction in any organization, a valuable lesson that put me on a course for my lifelong work with colleges.

CHANGE AND INNOVATION

Norm once said, "True education verifies experiences and opens us to new ideas and practices," emphasizing the importance of innovation and the readiness to accept change. I can only imagine his shock and pride as he listened to a team of visiting professors at UW refer to the very change his father Ernie had championed three decades earlier on their Nebraskan farm.

> *Norm:* My graduate studies tapped into what I'd learned from my father about the inevitability of change and how to stay ahead of the curve. Remarkably, the adoption of hybrid seed corn was a key focus in a presentation I heard twenty-five years later by Iowa State College professors Joe Bohlen and George Beale, entitled "How Ideas Get Adopted."
>
> They studied the long delay in the adoption of hybrid seed corn by American farmers in the early '30s. Geneticists had produced this marvelous new seed and expected a run on it, but instead they could not get rid of it. In fact, they discovered it would take more than thirteen years from the time they made it available before the majority of Iowa farmers planted hybrid seed. In their recounting of all the reasons those neighboring farmers gave for not adopting the hybrid corn, I heard almost word-for-word what my father heard twenty-five years earlier.
>
> That study presented by Bohlen and Beale reinforced my own experiences which were teaching me that if you want to get new things done, you must have a sense of delayed gratification and patience. Plant the seeds, water them, and wait until the time is right. If your ideas are not adopted, simply put them on the back burner, making sure to keep them warm. Adopt a stance toward progress, giving credit to others even though you know where the idea really originated. You may need to remove your ego to let others believe it was their idea in order to make it happen.

WHEN YOU ARE FINISHED CHANGING, YOU'RE FINISHED.
—BENJAMIN FRANKLIN

Norm must have felt the brakes stepped on when another professor announced to his class, "There is nothing new under the sun." This irritated him so much that it would be thirty years before he understood it, after observing the same problems emerge and reemerge both in work and greater society. He learned that the task was to find what is already present, understand it, use it, or possibly control it.

MASTER'S RESEARCH: A HEART THAT BELONGED TO EQUALITY

I'll never forget the stroll I took with my father through a sunlit path near the cut flower garden at Brandon Oaks Retirement Center, when, after knowing him all my life, I learned something new and surprising. While I knew higher education had been his calling, I didn't know how much his heart had belonged to ending racial injustice. This I discovered when he told me about his master's degree research project. *Think no little thoughts*, echoed in my mind as I listened.

His research had zeroed in on determining the root cause of racial discrimination and what the church, in particular the Lutheran Church, was doing about it. To understand the problem through the eyes of both the black and white "man on the street," he drove to Chicago where he interviewed anyone and everyone in one of the most racially divided areas of downtown, a section known as the "black belt" along Michigan Boulevard.

He walked those streets in 1959 when the burgeoning civil rights movement began to boil over, a year after Martin Luther King Jr. was stabbed at a book signing in Harlem and after King would march the streets in India, following in the footsteps of Mahatma Gandhi, calling for the weapon of nonviolence.

NORM'S THESIS TOPIC

Norm: Racism was hounding me. I had no clue. For my master's research project, I chose to answer this question: What influence does the church and religion have in combating and lessening the lines of discrimination, segregation, and prejudice of races?

I knew that if I wanted to understand the problem, I needed to be in the heart of it, so I went to Chicago. I parked my car on State St., locked the doors, and started to walk up and down the streets of a black ghetto neighborhood, stopping to talk to anyone who would speak to me.

My experience made me see that there were going to be big problems and there needed to be discussion. And we had to figure out a way to deal with it.

On my way downtown on Michigan Boulevard, I came across the offices of the Johnson Publishing company, home of the African-American magazine *Ebony*. I walked up rickety stairs to interview three African-American founders of the publication. Ed Clayton, associate editor in charge of religious copy, gave not only his own viewpoint but that of a number of other publications on the African-American viewpoint on religion and its influence. His view was that the church and religion were failing in finding a solution to the problem, fulfilling only primary church functions, and not daring to go beyond the extent of alleviating the prejudice, discrimination, and segregation to which they must fundamentally be opposed.

Of the *Ebony* articles I reviewed, two were of special interest. One was on Lutherans who were hesitant among African Americans because they had always opposed Jim Crow laws, and one on the Quakers because they were the only group that had come to grips with the problem and were taking immediate and practical steps toward the elimination of discrimination.

In another interview at the Third District Police Station, it was a sinking experience when the captain gave a response that was more typical of the attitude of white Chicagoans: "The problem is out of our hands, we have nothing to do with it."

The attitude of one white housewife is probably most indicative of many. She told me, "I'm not prejudiced, but when they talk of intermarriage I draw the line. I believe in keeping our blood pure. Why, it's proven that intermarriage has resulted in the downfall of nations because it deteriorated the race."

My conclusions were that we had immense problems, and I was convinced that church and religion in general are falling down miserably on the job. The hatred and despair generated by decades of slavery and discrimination is a deep, dark stain on the heart and soul of the African Americans, and a sharp, biting pin stuck in the conscience of the white. Neither face the problem directly, instead fueling resentment as blacks become more educated to what they are missing, and whites continue to save their conscience with the halfhearted belief that they are biologically better, anyway. Both ignore the power and all-healing love of God. Nor can one but cast a scathing indictment upon our own Lutheran Church for failing to take steps toward the solution of so fundamental a problem.

Tomorrow will not see the elimination of the race problem, nor will the next day, but I feel that the utter despair and desolation mirrored in the words, expressions, and publications of the African Americans cannot be relieved so long as people do not basically believe in the equality of all people. Perhaps in the eyes of most, the barrier is insurmountable, and if this is true, then it is but the first spin of a vicious circle that offers no solution but that of more spin to a wheel that will eventually explode from its own momentum.

What did I learn? I came to conclusion that Chicago and major cities are ripe for uprising. This was 1959.

FAITH IS TAKING THE FIRST STEP,
EVEN IF YOU DON'T SEE THE WHOLE STAIRCASE.
—MARTIN LUTHER KING JR.

Martin Luther King Jr.'s call for the weapon of nonviolence resonated with Norm. I knew this to be true from a lifetime of my father switching TV stations whenever violence was on the screen, not wanting to be exposed or expose his family to so much of it. I was reminded later in life, while talking with a neighbor at Brandon Oaks Retirement Center about how my father did a jigsaw puzzle. Both were avid puzzlers, but Betty said Norm quietly refused to work on the puzzle parts where soldiers were at battle. He was a pacifist to his core.

RETURN TO WARTBURG

With graduate school nearing the finish line, Norm sensed the winds of change in the air. When his new degree was in hand, he and Jo packed the car and drove home to Wartburg College in Waverly, Iowa.

Norm: The University of Wisconsin was absolutely the best place for me and for what I wanted to learn. It was hard, but it was fun. My experience confirmed what I had been learning and doing back on the job. It gave me a renewed sense of confidence that my life and career were on the right track. I was 34. I returned to Wartburg ready to do some planning and devise a strategy to make our college the best ever.

Change was brewing for all the Lutheran churches and colleges while Norm was in graduate school, and he was primed to take it on. But just as he returned to Wartburg to his old job, another door opened, beckoning him to take yet another path.

> *Norm:* I went back to Wartburg at a time when several synods of the Lutheran Church had just agreed to merge by January of 1961. Dr. Sidney Rand was hired to oversee the new church headquarters. Because I had just learned about management and how new ideas are adopted, I was more than a little interested in how this merger would change our work at Wartburg.
>
> My first act back on campus was to see President Becker and ask him about the impending merger of the Norwegian and German branches of the Lutheran Church, and what this meant for how we operated as a college. Wartburg was as German as could be! I asked how we would protect our German Lutheran heritage at the same time that we were recruiting the Norwegians to join us.
>
> I suggested to Dr. Becker that we interview Rand to find out how things were going to be run in this new church. It was going to be a new ballgame, and we would have to deal with it. I gave him some examples of what might change, but Dr. Becker shoved the matter aside with the comment that it really did not make much difference: *The Church will be the Church!* He *harrumphed* a little bit, passing it off as just another "Church thing," trying to run us from a distance.
>
> I felt rebuffed but had the temerity to ask if he would mind if I went to interview the new executive to see just how policies and procedures might change. He did not, so I went to Minneapolis to interview Dr. Rand, using what I had learned in graduate school.
>
> I learned in no uncertain terms that, contrary to business as usual, we in the colleges were in a new era. Rand

told me he wanted to run a service for the institutions—not the institutions themselves. It would be a new day of less interference, more competition, and greater emphasis on strong college leadership.

I came back and told Dr. Becker that it would be a new day and we ought to prepare for it. The news fell on deaf ears. However, I did change my strategies for my department—by then, I had personnel for admissions and publications and publicity.

The Spirit opened another door when in April 1960, Rand called me, asking if I would consider an interview for the position of one of his two assistants. My asking the right questions and his needing someone from the German side of the church had put me in the right place at the right time.

My horizons were about to expand. With absolutely no hesitation, I accepted Sidney Rand's job offer as the new assistant director of the board of college education. My salary was $8,000, up from $4,200 at Wartburg.

Once again, Jo and I loaded the Studebaker, now with three toddlers, and were off to Minnesota. I loved it, though!

QUESTIONS FOR SELF-REFLECTION

- Was there a time in your life when you struggled? How did you respond? Were there benefits from the hardship?
- In your late 20s and early 30s, did you understand the importance of being open to change? Do you have an example of how you were open and/or how you resisted it? Are you open to change today?
- Lifelong learning was part of Norm's life. How is lifelong learning threaded into your life? Do you think it is necessary for rising in your career? What are barriers to lifelong learning? How can you work around them?

CHAPTER 8

Branching Out

THE WINDS OF CHANGE (1960–1965)

LUCK IS WHAT HAPPENS WHEN PREPARATION MEETS OPPORTUNITY.
—SENECA

MOVING FROM SMALL TOWN LIFE in Nebraska and Iowa to navigating around two million people in Minneapolis must have been an eye-popping experience for Norm and Jo. When they couldn't afford a home in the city, they settled into a small western suburb, invitingly called Golden Valley. Peggy, Bill, and I, at ages four, three, and two, thrived in our big backyard with neighborhood children galore, top-rated schools, and safety in the streets. The caveat was that everyone in the neighborhood had lily-white skin.

No longer in charge of just one college, Norm now had charge of seventeen colleges scattered around the nation. He discovered a progressive-minded culture at the American Lutheran Church

(ALC) headquarters, where innovation and collaboration were thriving under the watchful leadership of Dr. Sidney Rand.

Norm stepped into the ALC when it was challenged by the lightning pace of change in the world of higher education and when it needed to be a steady influence on a nation finding itself on the edge. Political and civil unrest was ignited in the early '60s, and the assassination of President John F. Kennedy on November 22, 1963 shocked the world. Protesters marched the streets against the Vietnam War while civil rights' groundbreaking laws protected voters' rights, barring segregation and discrimination against race or gender. Norm's much needed "bring-your-values-to-work" ethic found a home at the crossroads of 5th Avenue and 5th Street, the ALC headquarters in Minneapolis.

He moved up the ladder quickly, establishing the backbone of his management and leadership philosophies while blazing the trail for the future. His experience is a reminder of what is possible when opportunity knocks on your door, and you trust enough to enter without a blink.

> *Norm:* My story is one of rags to riches, or from farm to leadership in education and the church. I was blessed to live by the spirit. I was a vehicle. As I look back, I can see that Spirit was leading me, but I did not understand that at the time. I just went on to do the best I could under the circumstances—in a sense, plowing and planting and nourishing the soil to unleash the abundance of life.
>
> As Jo settled the kids into our new home nestled in the suburban community of Golden Valley, I began commuting into the city to the ALC offices.
>
> With this new opportunity, I was closer to my ambition to educate young people, getting them to think for themselves, to take leadership roles and be the power within their families, careers, and larger society.
>
> Honesty, integrity, trustworthiness, and *agape* love [the highest form of love: charity] are the keys to living with joy

and purpose. These values guided my life both at home and in work. Values drive "true" success and define the work of a leader. Leadership is all about character and consistency, doing well for others and yourself. First, you have to be the leader in your own life.

NORM'S LIFE LESSON #20

EXPECT UPS AND DOWNS, AND LEARN FROM EACH EXPERIENCE SO THE NEXT TIME IS EASIER. "I'M WILLING TO TRY ANYTHING TWICE: THE FIRST TIME I MIGHT HAVE MISSED SOMETHING."

EMBRACING CHANGE: THE AMERICAN LUTHERAN CHURCH YEARS

Colleges were in trouble at the start of the 1960s, and Rand's team set about rescuing their own. Keeping budgets in the black and making education affordable were problems on a scale similar to those today. Help didn't arrive until 1965 when the Higher Education Act strengthened funding and financial assistance to students.

Embracing change became Norm's strategy for turning around the church colleges, a perfect opportunity for Norm to practice what he learned from his father and at the University of Wisconsin.

Norm: I realized things were changing, but I couldn't always tell you why or in what direction and what role we, as a church and higher education in the church, ought to play in order to help things change. The agony of our urban crisis said very loudly, *Do something!*

We dealt with the cascading changes in higher education, causing record setting enrollment and an expansion of traditional curriculum. A new breed of leadership was needed, moving away from choosing clergy or faculty to be college presidents. This all came with a price tag, leading up to too many of the seventeen ALC colleges operating in the red and an alarming $1.5 million combined loss in one year alone.

As more college presidents started looking for answers, our phone started ringing. This put our work on a fast track, and innovation was the name of the game. Our single largest challenge was how to help these colleges keep up with the times. We developed and ran management and leadership training conferences for presidents, deans, financial officers, chaplains, and administrators in PR, development, admissions, alumni—virtually for any group that wanted to be in on change.

Without fully realizing it, my appetite for "how things get done" was insatiably whetted. My real training for management leadership had begun. I learned how you get down to what really matters. How to do it, and how to know if it works.

MENTORS AND A GLOBAL PERSPECTIVE

Norm's counterpart was Loren Halverson, Dr. Rand's assistant director of social research. Loren exposed Norm to a global perspective and grassroots cultural development practices, and taught him a valuable lesson in leadership that served him well throughout his career.

Norm: Loren's fertile mind and boundless spirit simply could not be stalled. He had been influential in helping the Germans recover from World War II and rebuild a society through educational systems that had meaning and value. He understood how to change a whole culture. I mean a *total* culture.

He brought about change through leadership of the real workers—the lay people, not the clergy. His team tackled problems identified by the masses of German people, such as *How did this happen to us? Why did we let the Nazis do this? Why did we abandon the church so quickly?*

Loren and I went on to start a similar lay movement for change in the U.S. built around our Lutheran Church colleges. Later we would travel to Germany, where I had a deepening of my understanding of cultural development.

A lasting impression Loren left on me was his favored leadership technique, which he termed "enabling them through absence." He enabled the real workers—the people—to take ownership of whatever project they were on and get it done. He would stir up the crew, then leave the room to let them work out a plan. I've used this strategy throughout my career, and it works. It creates a movement by the people, for the people. People own it.

NORM'S LIFE LESSON #21

SOLUTIONS ARE DISCOVERED WHEN PEOPLE TAKE OWNERSHIP OF THE PROCESS. "A LEADER PLANTS SEEDS AND STIRS THE POT."

Working with Sid and Loren in these early years of the 1960s was an exciting and challenging time of evolution, one which I have not seen paralleled in more recent American institutional life. The same vibrancy of leadership and the openness to change would not be seen throughout the rest of my career.

Little did Norm know that Rand was being groomed for a position as the president of one of the Lutheran colleges. When Rand left for St. Olaf College in Northfield, Minnesota, the executive director position at ALC opened up for Norm. And little did I know how much Loren Halverson's lesson on building a grass roots, bottom-up culture would be passed down to me in my work with Dining for Women, an organization that thrives with this kind of collaborative culture.

EARLY YEARS AS EXECUTIVE DIRECTOR

As the new executive director, Norm led his team to create what they referred to as "management audits," the purpose of which was to find solutions for turning around both colleges and their leadership. They were plowing new territory, realizing that what worked for one college was not necessarily the solution for another. It was also where Norm fell in love with problem solving and came to identify himself as an "eclectic pragmatic."

A snapshot of these management audits demonstrates why personal values are necessary for successfully leading change and modernization. The same three questions Norm asked Wartburg students in his initial speech as director for admissions and public relations became a strategy for the management audit process. A values-driven work ethic emerged.

> *Norm:* When a college president asked the ALC for help, we sent a management audit team of four experts who spent three days examining the balance of the team in place, how and why it worked or did not work. We led them through developing and using long range plans. In every case, we improved the effectiveness of the college.
>
> Our philosophy was simple and pragmatic. It boiled down to three simple questions which became the backbone of all our work.
>
> 1. What needs to be done?
> 2. What keeps you from doing it?
> 3. Where do we begin?
>
> The answers to these three questions act like a GPS, mapping out how to get to where you want to be. How

do you get down to what really matters, where real change occurs? Then follow-up by evaluating if the strategy is working, and if not, why not.

We knew that good leadership was essential and carefully instilled in college leaders the sense that uncovering one's weaknesses is a sign of strength if those weaknesses are addressed and changes made. Prominent psychologists said that if a person had not developed the mechanism for change and adaptation by age forty, there was little hope of expecting change later in life. To really address change then, one must address the subjects before they have reached the hardening stage. We knew we must have open-minded professors and administrators.

NORM'S LIFE LESSON #22

A FISH STINKS FIRST IN THE HEAD! IF YOU'RE NOT WILLING TO CHANGE, WE HAVE A PROBLEM.

We also realized that down deep, management reflects the values and skills of an individual, values that are key to successful leadership. We defined four essential values: *honesty, integrity, trustworthiness,* and *agape love.* These were same values which shaped my own development from my youth.

As our audit team gained confidence and our reputation spread, invitations came from more and more colleges. We did some thirty to forty audits before my career took me on another adventure.

Our beliefs give us an internal guiding system, similar to how the gyroscope is used in planes as an automatic pilot system. But this system as a set of personal values is not enough. I believe one must also have an understanding of human nature. In other words, the world as it really is *versus* the world that we think ought to be. In simple words, leadership is all about character and values and consistency.

THERE ARE THREE CONSTANTS IN LIFE—
CHANGE, CHOICE, AND PRINCIPLES.
—STEPHEN COVEY

IMMERSION AND CONSCIOUS BIAS TRAINING

While the audits were ticking along at the ALC, civil unrest demanded action from the Church and our country. There were student sit-ins at lunch counters in Greensboro, NC. There was Martin Luther King Jr.'s March on Washington, where he told us "I Have a Dream" and another shocking assassination, this time of Malcom X on February 21, 1965. Rioting was going on in the streets of Los Angeles. A rallying cry for leadership landed at President Johnson's front door leading to the Great Society social reforms for poverty and racial injustice.

Norm: Racism and inequality go hand in hand. The imperative for us all dates back to the Old Testament where the central issue was the freedom of life for each individual. An example of intolerance is seen in early civilizations—the Arabs, Medes, and Persians—where each clan seems to be more and more concerned about being right. Absolutely right. And therefore, absolutely wrong. When one clan claims they, and they alone, know the truth, they become intolerant of the freedom to hold another view. Freedom of life for each individual cannot exist where intolerance is the rule.

One step the ALC took to combat the growing racial division was to give its staff a sensitivity training.

> *Norm:* Over the years Jo and I committed ourselves to ending discrimination. The Church did, too. Race riots were closing the doors of schools and universities. Something needed to be done.
>
> By the mid-'60s, management seminars and retreats were the rage. In 1964, a week of sensitivity training transformed my life, and subsequently those in my family. I learned what I wasn't doing right in all facets of life.
>
> The ALC sent thirty-five managers to American University in Washington, DC, for three weeks of training to help us deal with the forces of unconscious bias, and to discern the signs and symptoms of discrimination within society. I came home and told Jo I was a new person, and I needed for her to learn with me how to deal with all the changes we needed to make. One of these would be to move back into the city of Minneapolis to help fill the leadership vacuum caused in part by "white flight."

Another door was about to open, and by walking through it Norm would again allow himself to be led by Spirit. He was living his faith and trusting that a move out of the suburbs and into the city was what he and his family needed to do.

I recall my father once saying of my mother, "Jo does not see color." I would add my mother meant that she recognized the beauty in different races and cultures, but didn't discern those differences as boundaries in humankind, whether race, religion, gender, socio-economic class, or any other label that would separate herself from others. He didn't, either.

NORM'S LIFE LESSON #23

ACTIONS SPEAK LOUDER THAN WORDS.
DON'T TALK THE WALK—WALK IT.

QUESTIONS FOR SELF-REFLECTION

- Think about ways you take your values to work. Does your employer identify company values? If so, what ways are those woven into your responsibilities and the work you do?
- For Norm, the predominant social issue was equality. What is the predominant social issue you feel passionate about? In what ways are you "walking the talk?"

CHAPTER 9

Transplanting

A BOLD MOVE OF MORAL LEADERSHIP
(1966–1970)

IT IS VITAL THAT WHEN EDUCATING OUR CHILDREN'S BRAINS, WE DO NOT NEGLECT TO EDUCATE THEIR HEARTS.
—THE DALAI LAMA

IN THE MID-1960S, MY FATHER EXPERIENCED AN A-HA MOMENT of unshakeable faith, and our lives changed with one of his most courageous, noble decisions. The family said goodbye to lily-white Golden Valley, the neighborhood everyone dreams of living in, and transplanted to inner-city Minneapolis. It was a move that placed us in the heart of an integrated neighborhood, woven with every color of the tapestry of life. By then, Peggy, Bill, and I were at the very impressionable ages of ten, nine, and eight.

Brewing societal discontent spilled over in the late '60s, spurring an infectious rallying cry for change. People took to the streets protesting the

Vietnam War, equal rights for women, and racial discrimination. Societal frustration was expressed through blaring rock and roll, long hair, bell bottoms, and love beads, like those worn by Mr. Johnson, my sister Peggy's new 6th grade teacher.

This chapter explores what is possible when your faith cannot be shaken and when sparks from an equal-partnership marriage bring about a magical harmony to make bold decisions work. My father's relentless quest for righting wrongs can inspire each of us to believe that we, too, can make a difference.

A BOLD MOVE

Somewhere along the way, as Norm commuted to and from the inner city to our suburban home or maybe when he traveled the country, a light bulb switched on, illuminating the path to his next step. It became clear that he needed to be where racial disharmony was rampant, where change must begin, the inner city of Minneapolis.

When John Mason, a colleague at the American Lutheran Church, mentioned to Norm there was an affordable house for sale near him in the city, another door swung open, one that might have been lit by a neon sign saying *Walk This Way*. Our family said goodbye to shocked neighbors and to the safety-net of Golden Valley, and our lives were never the same. For the three of us kids, to say our eyes were opened during this next phase of our lives would be a gross understatement.

> *Norm:* By the mid-'60s, I had made up my mind I was not going to live in a way that expressed any bias toward others. I was a changed person.
>
> Jo and I agreed that in order to help fix the problem, we needed to be where the problem was. In 1966, we moved from the suburbs to the inner city to help fill the leadership vacuum caused in part by what was known as "white flight." We moved toward the problem rather than stay out in the white suburbs.

White flight began before there was violence and tension, before the student riots over equal rights. Those with wealth and education escaped to the suburbs; instead of whites taking leadership, they said let's get out of here and let them run it. They were escapists, and I objected to that.

The benefit of the move was a clear conscience from being part of the solution, not part of the problem. I didn't have a plan of what to do. I just thought that white people should be in there, in the trenches fighting with everyone else. It worked for us, but it wasn't for everyone. But for me, I am confronting this issue in my work and in what was happening in the world around us, and I thought, *If we don't do it, who will?*

NORM'S LIFE LESSON #24

ABOVE ALL, ALWAYS SEARCH FOR THE TRUTH.
IF YOU SEE A WRONG, MAKE IT RIGHT.
LIVE WITH A SENSE OF URGENCY
OR NOTHING EVER CHANGES.

By living where racial discord was splattered over the daily news, we three children were exposed to all spectrums of real life. We moved into our fourth home—2522 38th Avenue South in Minneapolis in 1966, near but not in the most heavily blighted neighborhoods. It was a big house, built in the early 1900s, and needed much attention. There was a garage in the alley, a second rental house on the rear of the property, and the Mississippi River right across the street. My brother Bill describes our new surroundings:

Bill Fintel: The move to the city at this time was one that went in the opposite direction for suburban-bound, upwardly mobile Americans. We three children had had it all, a flat grassy backyard, great public schools, best friends in every direction, and safety in the streets, such that Halloween meant free movement in any direction and the virtual assurance of coming home unmolested. Yet my father felt the best way for his children to see the vast richness of life was for us to move where the quilt had more colors.

PARENTING IN THE INNER CITY

My parents taught us through example, like my father's parents had done for him. We had few spoken rules, but we always knew exactly what was expected of us.

Peggy, Bill, and I were given a long leash to experiment, to figure out who we were and what we stood for. Mistakes were considered learning opportunities and taught us resilience. We were expected to think for ourselves and taught not to make assumptions or rush to judgment. We were taught to question the rules, respectfully, that everyone is created equal, and to follow the *Golden Rule*. Most importantly, we learned to run toward problems, not away from them.

I remember the freedom we had, often being given a quarter for the city bus on a Saturday morning after chores. Bill and I would explore every store and walkway downtown. Once I remember riding that bus all the way to the end of its route, just to see where it went. I'm sure no one knew I did that. Such freedom sparked a flame for curiosity and experimentation that opened my mind to what might be possible, a precursor that shaped my own work of making a difference on a global scale later on.

I took advantage of this freedom more than Peggy or Bill did, and now and then my rebellious streak got me into trouble. As the youngest child, no one paid much attention to me. I had a bike, bus money, and not many rules. I grew fiercely independent, a fearless explorer. Brackett Park, Minnehaha Falls, Dinky Town, the banks of the Mississippi, and a favorite, the downtown public library, a place that was so huge I had to go up and down on escalators in order to learn about whatever I wanted.

Norm's long-leash parenting style continued with his grandchildren. Anytime they left the house to go out with friends, they remember him saying: "Be good, and if you can't be good, have fun!"

> *Norm:* As parents, we didn't tell our children when to come home; we'd ask when they wanted to be in. We'd say, okay, and then they'd be here. They learned you didn't need to break the law to have fun. Each of them needed to develop their own faith and understanding. We didn't insist on doing the right thing; instead we'd ask them what the right thing to do was.

With work taking my father all over the country, we had my mom raising us on the daily home front. And, oh what a mom she was! A rebel, educator, and lover of the underdog, she was a feminist before that label was ever heard. She had an uncanny aptitude for drilling down to the heart of people and their problems, and to speak common sense. She was known for detecting falsehoods and calling them out as "bullshit." She taught us to speak up for ourselves. We loved her.

> *Norm:* Because I traveled so much during the children's formative years, Jo shouldered the parenting and teaching responsibilities as naturally as her own mother had done. Besides influencing the children, Jo took classes at St. Thomas College, volunteered at Fairview Hospital, served on the Board of the Home for Unwed Mothers, taught Sunday School, and led her daughters' Girl Scout Troop.

IT'S TIME FOR PARENTS TO TEACH YOUNG PEOPLE EARLY ON THAT IN DIVERSITY THERE IS BEAUTY AND THERE IS STRENGTH.

—MAYA ANGELOU

I once asked my mother why she was a feminist. Her response: "Off the top of my head, I don't know why. Sometimes my mouth gets me in trouble." Or maybe it began at a young age, when she and her own mother were always at loggerheads. "I couldn't dance, smoke, carouse—all were considered sinful." In my brother Bill's words:

> *Bill Fintel:* She was and is a teacher and wrote in our hearts and minds all the principles my father was teaching. But she also attended to the many finer arts of life, giving us music lessons, having us attend Sunday School and choir, and teaching us to value the importance of family for everyone, especially the elderly and underdogs in life. She did this while my father was off to save the world and sometimes gone as much as 60 percent of the time. She kept us fed, clean, loved, and saw to it that we were off to school on time. We never missed church on Sunday. To this day, my parents' love and guidance keeps me "out of the ditches."

Looking back at this time, it's clear to me how I got where I am today in my life, and why I traveled the roads I'd chosen. Back roads, side roads, and my favorite gravel roads, sometimes taking me to the most remote areas of the world where I have been privileged to make a difference in people's lives through Dining for Women.

NAVIGATING-INNER CITY SCHOOLS

My mother was a teacher, so navigating the public school system of the inner city came naturally to her. Our new schools exposed us to the full spectrum of real life. She tells about her impressions when enrolling us at our new school in the inner city:

> *Jo:* As I was sitting in the secretary's office at Seward Elementary School, waiting to register the kids in 3rd, 4th, and 5th

> grade, in walked this short, stocky man to check his mail box, sporting an immense beard and wearing love beads, and I am thinking to myself, *Oh no, what have we gotten into... I hope my kids don't get him!* Then Peggy got assigned to that very teacher, Mr. Johnson, and I ended up liking him so much, I requested him for both Bill and Barb over the next two years.

On my first day of school at Seward, I found a note on my desk challenging me to meet on the playground for a fight after school. I showed up, but the challenger did not. Later she and I became fast friends.

In the classroom, there was every color and every creed sitting at the desks. I learned to stand up for myself and not back away from challenges, to look on the inside rather than the outside, and to delay judgment until I got the facts.

I began honing my individuality by testing the boundaries of acceptance by the "in-crowd," choosing to often follow the beat of my own drummer. I took my freedom to the edge many times but always pulled back before finding myself in any real trouble.

Our next public school was Sanford Jr. High on 35th Street and 42nd Avenue South. It was too far to walk, and there were no school buses, so we rode the city bus. My mother describes those days from her viewpoint:

> *Jo:* At Sanford Jr. High, Peggy went to her first class where her social studies teacher, Mr. Bucanagua (American Indian descent) told her he didn't give A's to girls. From then on, she was determined to show him, and show him she did, and most every teacher that followed, always graduating first in her class.

Later, when I had Mr. Bucanagua as my teacher, he never let us forget he was a former boxer and made us all practice right jabs fifty times, over and over. He tried to get under my skin when he called us up one by one to get our report cards. I opened mine to see a D. He watched my reaction before calling me back up to change it to a B, the result of which was to thicken my skin for the future.

From my mother, I learned to question the rules and change them if they needed it. Back then, girls still wore dresses to school, no matter if the temperature was twenty degrees below zero. We'd wear pants under our dresses, so we wouldn't freeze while waiting for the bus to and from school. One day, my mother sent me without the mandatory dress, knowing full well it would create a ruckus. I was pulled into the principal's office and sent home, but the dress code was changed that year. Seeds of a rebel were planted.

NORM'S LIFE LESSON #25

RULES ARE MADE TO BE BROKEN.

Another pivotal experience for me was being assigned an 8th grade class track that placed me outside my circle of friends. My new friends exposed me to risky endeavors that my other friends wouldn't dare try. I developed as an outlier, occupying a place of comfort where I could learn a lot through observing human behavior. Once the three of us kids were headed to South High School, on 31st Street 19th Avenue South, our bus route changed, and we kept warm in a White Castle diner at the corner of where we had to transfer.

During those years, my father decided he would pursue a doctoral degree, so my mom returned to the classroom to help make ends meet. Jo found a position teaching learning-disabled students at one of the most challenging inner-city elementary schools further up on Lake Street. This experience gave her a ringside seat for seeing the differences between small town vs. urban school environments.

Jo: With the kids now old enough and Norm beginning to work on his doctorate, I returned to teaching. Because I already had nine years of teaching experience and would have commanded too high a salary, they wouldn't give me a classroom. So I applied for a position in special education and later returned to graduate school for a master's in special education.

At my interview with the personnel director of the Minneapolis schools, I waited as he sat there with my resume. He asked me, "Why do you think that coming from a small, rural college in Iowa, you could teach our inner-city kids?" I said, "I don't know, I just know I have a lot of love to give them." I was hired.

Much like Norm had experience at the ALC, I had to attend sensitivity trainings for my new position, to be a better teacher. First, I rode one night in a police car through the inner city. Then, another experience had me in a wheelchair at a shopping mall, learning from people's reactions when encountering someone with a disability.

My first student was Gus. He was black, standing six feet tall in the 6th grade. He had witnessed his father shoot a neighbor. All the teachers were afraid of him. One of my first days, he reached over and gave my hair a yank. I asked him: "Why did you do that?" He said he wanted to see if my hair was real or a wig.

I worked with him every day, even took him to our lake cabin with the family. Norm taught him how to chop wood. On the drive up north, we realized he didn't know how to read the sign with "exit" and didn't know what it meant. He had never been out of the city. Norm told him he might see a deer. I thought that wouldn't happen, though sure enough, a deer leaped across 35 W right in front of us.

On days I taught through art, Gus painted black dancers. When I complimented him on his painting, he told me it depicted the black national anthem. I was not aware there was one. I paid him $5 for the painting which has graced our wall ever since.

My mom's exposure to the city was different from my father's more insulated environment at the ALC. One night, Norm came home on the bus and said to Jo, "You know, I don't think people are swearing as much anymore." She told him, "You are dealing with the wrong people. At school I hear bad words every day that I've never heard of." He encouraged her to teach him this new language.

NORM'S LIFE LESSON #26

THERE IS LEARNING GOING ON AT EVERY SCHOOL. SOME TEACH MORE ABOUT REAL LIFE THAN OTHERS. PARENTAL INSTINCTS RUSH THEIR CHILDREN TO THE "BEST" SCHOOLS, DEFINED BY STANDARDIZED TESTS, BUT WE DON'T THINK ENOUGH ABOUT PREPARING STUDENTS FOR REAL LIFE.

Jo's rabble-rousing continued teaching us by example, as Peggy, Bill, and I attended South High.

Jo: When I attended a meeting of the South High PTA, South being a very poor school, I learned our school was sending $1,000 to the central PTA office for dues. So I got elected president, and we voted to become PUSH instead of PTA. This stood for Parents United for South High (Norm claims credit for the name), and our abandoning the bureaucracy of the parent offices and spending the money on more important things on the never-ending list for the school. We were offended by sending our money away and having no voice in how it was being spent. With a mile-long list of improvements needed at South, we needed every dime to improve education for our children.

Peggy and Bill coasted through high school earning straight A's, setting an impossible example for me, the youngest, to follow. I stayed true to the beat of a different drummer, despite wearing the uniform of a cheerleader. I lasted two years before turning in my uniform and finding comfort once again in my own skin.

Moving from the suburbs to city had lasting ramifications in all of our lives. Peggy and Bill have their own stories to tell. Peggy shares hers first.

Peggy Fintel Horn: I was the shy, scared little girl who grew up in Golden Valley surrounded by family and friends with no perceivable threats, and then was thrust into an inner-city elementary school with only my family as a safety net. What the experience gave me was an incredible view into the variety of life, a life-long friend who stood up in class and said she was my friend when I didn't even know her, and a love of anything that isn't quite normal.

To say my father was the backbone of the family was not entirely true. He was the moral compass, a quiet, thoughtful man who never told a lie. If he didn't have anything nice to say, he said nothing. It was his vibrant, outgoing wife who was the heart of the family. My mom made sure we all stayed on track.

I remember I wore a pink paisley dress with a little pink leather belt to my first day of fifth grade in the inner city. It was the last day I wore a dress to school. On that first day, Nancy Nelson stood up and told the teacher she knew me, because she had ridden her bike over to see the moving van show up at the house. She decided we would be friends, and she immediately made me a part of her circle.

When I think back to that move, I recall how I learned that the world was not all black and white, good and bad. I met people who forced me to open my eyes to the world and to think before I made assumptions. I learned I could swim in a bigger ocean, and I met people who challenged me. It could have happened in the suburbs because of the kind of family I came from, but I don't think I would have been as outgoing if I'd stayed tucked safely away. And because my father and mother trusted that we could survive and flourish anywhere, I learned that I could, as well. My parents thought the change to the inner-city schools opened up intellectual freedom where Bill would blossom. He agrees with that, and then some.

Bill Fintel: My new inner-city fourth grade elementary classroom included African Americans, Native Americans, and kids that didn't seem to bathe very often. There were also University of Minnesota professors' children and kids whose parents were criminals. Some of my new best friends had parents who taught English at the University, wrote hymns for the Lutheran hymnal, and served as missionaries in New Guinea. There was another whose father boasted a plastic replica of an outhouse with a door that opened, and the patron swung out and urinated exactly one shot of Vodka in your glass.

The move to the edge of the Mississippi River in Minneapolis exerted a long pull on my life. That river defined many aspects of American life and was like any river that moves you in ways you don't always understand. I loved the river and its bridges, and the death-defying walks on its frozen surface in January. I loved biking and running its trails and will always recall its majesty.

On a personal note, I am eternally grateful to my parents for leading me to Minneapolis public schools, and specifically South High School, where I met and fell hopelessly in love by the age of fifteen with a cheerleader who was friends with both my sisters.

For me, I remember feeling a heightened sense of alert as soon as I took in my new surroundings in third grade. It wasn't fear, rather inquisitiveness as multi-colored faces replaced the all-white. With so many walks of life to understand, it freed me to explore who I might want to be. I tested the boundaries of this freedom and dipped my toe into water which might have pulled me under, were it not for the safety net of values embedded in me by my parents. I was in my own process of becoming with my own "hole waiting to be filled." In one of my last conversations with my father, we spoke about this time:

Mom: You were always a rebel.
Me: I was. I wonder where I got that.
Dad: Your mother.

THE TRUTH IS LIVED, NOT TAUGHT.
—HERMANN HESSE

FAMILY TRAVEL

Our exposure to real life continued as our father traveled thousands and thousands of miles across the country to visit Lutheran campuses. Whenever possible, he traded airfare for gas money and took the family along, opening our eyes to a world beyond our backyard. We'd drive all night, the kids sleeping in the backseat, saving the cost of a hotel room. One memorable trip took us south when Martin Luther King Jr. was assassinated. Bill shares the story of this rich learning experience.

Bill Fintel: Most eleven-year-olds look forward to spring break, especially when the snow piles are still part of life, as it was for us Minnesotans. So when my father said we were going south over the break, it made perfect sense, although little did I know how this trip would affect me for the rest of my life.

The battle for civil rights in America was in full swing. The assassination of Martin Luther King Jr. gripped the nation and coincided with our automobile journey. The five of us recall seeing the black and white police cars swarming as we drove through Memphis. We felt awed by touching a piece of that moment in history by driving through that city when the world was erupting.

My father led us farther south with the guise of making it to the Gulf of Mexico, and indeed we stayed in a motel right on the Gulf like any other tourists. But the morality play he was writing in our hearts went far past avoiding snow storms or playing in warm sand. He drove past several laundromats with signs that read *Whites Only*, and showed us drinking fountains that said the same.

On Easter morning, we five, snow-white Fintels walked into a non-white, steepled church and communed with brothers and sisters we didn't know. I still remember the enormous smiles that greeted us as we walked into that church. I can only imagine what the congregants were thinking. But fresh on the heels of the assassination of the most famous African American of our times, these people of color treated us like family! The fact that this is a nearly fifty-year-old memory and still resonates speaks to the huge impact that experience had on me.

NORM'S LIFE LESSON #27

LOOK AROUND AND GET OUTSIDE OF YOUR OWN BACKYARD. GO TO THE HEART OF THE PROBLEM, SEE IT FOR WHAT IT IS AND TALK IT OUT.

CLOSING ON MINNEAPOLIS AND MINNESOTA

Beyond city schools, we were exposed by our parents to the many colors within our inner-city neighborhood. We brought food to Native-American families in need, living just over the Hiawatha railroad tracks. We worshiped with a black congregation up Lake Street. We learned to cook sukiyaki from a Korean neighbor renting the top floor of a home across the alley. Every Sunday, we attended Hope Lutheran Church, adjacent to Dinkytown, a trendy district on the north side of the University of Minnesota, with all shapes and sizes in the pews.

Beyond the city, I loved the state of Minnesota and consider it influential in my development as a social activist. I remember U.S. senator from Minnesota and 38th vice president Hubert Humphrey urging people to "get out of the shadows of states' rights and walk forthrightly into the bright sunshine of human rights." And who could grow up not loving Prince, Harmon Killebrew, or the butter sculptures at the State Fair? Lest we not forget Jessie Ventura wrestling his way to the Governor's mansion. Though it was native Judy Garland who got it all right when her character Dorothy said, "There's no place like home."

KIDS DESERVE THE RIGHT TO THINK
THAT THEY CAN CHANGE THE WORLD.
—LOIS LOWRY

SAND LAKE SUMMERS

After surviving winter, Minnesotans are crazy about their 20,000 lakes. Most everyone heads "up north" to find solace in the northern lights and the soulful call of the loon.

On my tenth birthday, we spent a week on Sand Lake, where friends had a cabin that was passed down through generations. On our last day, my parents impulsively bought a "need lots of work" cabin with a "worth the price" view for $5,000, fully furnished. It came with a pump in the kitchen for water we couldn't drink and a two-holer out back, a biffy with an exquisite view of the lake.

No TV, no phone, no heat, no reason to be inside. No rules, other than shut the door quickly to keep out the bugs, take the flashlight if you come home late, wear long sleeves when picking berries, and don't come home from the Fourth of July town fair unless you bring extra teeny-weeny donuts.

Our summers at Sand Lake were filled baiting hooks, cleaning fish, slathering on suntan oil, and hunting agates on the dirt road, waiting for our father to arrive every Friday night. For him, it was a place for nourishing the soul, where love and adventure were the catch of every day. His words capture the magic:

> *Norm:* It is wonderful to be here. The lake works its magic on both our spirits. Somehow, even in the rainy spells, we are more at peace. I suppose it is in part because we are not bothered by the busy demands of work, causes, friends and neighbors, or the social whirl. Not that those things aren't important to us, but sometimes we need the silence of retreat to remember who we really are. Like going to dinner with Bud and Marilyn last night, driving all the way to Finlayson on the old road, just to eat chicken for $4.95 (all you can eat).

NORM'S LIFE LESSON #28

DON'T FORGET TO SLOW DOWN AND
ENJOY THE BEAUTY OF THE EARTH.
WE ALL MUST BE ITS GUARDIANS.

When opening his whole heart on his quest for equality, Norm brought us all along in the search for solutions. I have no doubt his own father would have said, *Well done, son. You didn't just stand there—you did something.*

QUESTIONS FOR SELF-REFLECTION

- Norm and Jo's hands-off, modeling style of parenting is not the norm today. How would you describe your parenting style? How long is the leash of freedom for your children?
- What are the values you want or have instilled within your children? What were the most effective methods for teaching them?
- Norm's commitment to equality and education began early. What social issues are most important to you, and how did they come to be meaningful to you? What do you do to advance these causes?

CHAPTER 10

Cross Pollination

FORMING A GLOBAL VISION
(1970–1975)

MORAL AUTHORITY COMES FROM UNIVERSAL AND TIMELESS PRINCIPLES, LIKE HONESTY, INTEGRITY, TREATING PEOPLE WITH RESPECT.
—STEPHEN COVEY

IN HIS LATER YEARS AT THE AMERICAN LUTHERAN CHURCH HEADQUARTERS, Norm settled in as the management audits continued to reshape and reinforce the foundational bases of the seventeen colleges, anchoring them in moral-based leadership. While my mother navigated the family, my father's surging quest for knowledge and truth sent him back to the classroom where another door opened for him to learn from yet another a master.

This was a time of escalating discontent with the leadership in our country and with our involvement in the Vietnam War. College campuses reeled with the deaths of four student war protesters at Kent State. Then the nation lost trust in its president when a scandal exposed Nixon's connection to breaking into the Democratic National Committee headquarters at Watergate. We watched as Nixon tried to cover his tracks, only to fail and have to resign in disgrace.

With a growing sense of urgency that was fueled by a trip through Germany, Norm's eyes were opened to the necessity of preparing the next generation of moral leaders while bringing a global vision into the world of academia.

SERVANT LEADERSHIP

I can almost see my dad driving along with the car windows down, wind in his hair, crisscrossing the county to visit ALC's many colleges with plenty of time and freedom to think. What better time to ponder leadership, evolution, and the meaning of faith.

From the years of evaluating leadership through management and board audits, it was natural he would turn to the wisdom of a Midwesterner like himself and founder of the modern servant leadership movement, Robert Greenleaf.

Greenleaf's premise, based on his research in management and education, was that the power-centered authoritarian leadership style so prominent in U.S. institutions was not working, and a new model was needed. He was influenced by Hermann Hesse, one of Norm's early influencers, a German whose mystical tales in *The Journey to the East* first promoted the idea of a leader who was effective because he served his followers first. Greenleaf's many publications still grace our bookshelves.

THE SERVANT LEADER IS SERVANT FIRST... THEN CONSCIOUS CHOICE BRINGS ONE TO ASPIRE TO LEAD. THAT PERSON IS SHARPLY DIFFERENT THAN ONE WHO IS LEADER FIRST.

—ROBERT K. GREENLEAF

Norm: Servanthood is enabling others—your institution—to move ahead to where you all want to be. This concept is helpful in steering away from the traps of ego, pride, and arrogance. Doing the right thing for the right reason still pays off.

Greenleaf makes the point that there are always leaders and always followers, that a leader is made by followers. He considers servant leaders as "prophetic voices of great clarity." This type of leader "grows in stature as people responded to his message." (Quoted from Greenleaf's book *The Servant Leader*)

Norm also spent considerable time studying the work of Pierre Teilhard de Chardin, a visionary existentialist, biologist, paleontologist, and French priest considered radical in his time. Chardin opened his eyes and kept him from falling into the trap of narrow thinking, affecting him in a parallel way as had his parents and his childhood mentor, Pastor Schwerin.

One example is Chardin's early 1920s stance on evolution during a time when religious leaders believed evolution challenged the very structure of traditional Christian faith. Chardin's book, *The Phenomenon of Man*, posthumously published in 1955, described the unfolding of the evolution of humanity, abandoning literal interpretations of creation as told in the Bible in favor of allegorical interpretations.

Norm: Once I was introduced to Chardin, I was hooked. He spent the bulk of his life trying to integrate religion with science, most specifically, theories of evolution. His mystical, scientific, and religious approach spoke to me.

I read all his books, understanding little but thinking a lot about the faith we have without ever knowing God. It comes down to a leap in faith. Though we are often discouraged, and many give up, those that trust in God's wisdom and power will ultimately be rewarded and may in fact make a difference. Faith gives us confidence and a fearlessness to act out our values, though it's easier to let fear justify our inaction.

NORM'S LIFE LESSON #29

OPEN YOUR MIND TO POSSIBILITIES.

"THE MIND IS A HOLE WAITING TO BE FILLED."

CONTINUED EDUCATION

In 1971, the spirit appeared to guide Norm once again, as yet another door opened on his greater mission, one he would walk through in spite of any personal thoughts he might have about doing so. At age forty-three, he biked across the Mississippi River, just miles from our home, and entered a classroom at the University of Minnesota.

The ALC had given him a one-year, paid sabbatical to start his doctoral studies, so he began this time with his wallet fairly intact. In a chance encounter with Minnesota's Governor Elmer Andersen, who he happened to be sitting next to on an airplane, a conversation led to further funding from Andersen's personal foundation and a reference letter if Norm ever needed one.

Norm: These post-war times of societal discord were full of radical, challenging change. Being thrust into a new dimension of leadership, dealing with more and more presidents and deans who had Ph.D.s, I felt a need to earn the ticket, less for its own sake than for the satisfaction that I could then be better heard. No matter, the title of "Dr." made a difference.

I began classes, going nights and weekends and then got a year sabbatical from the ALC. This time, at the University of Minnesota, I was learning about organizations and how they did or did not work. At Wisconsin, I had learned more about people and cultures, and how to work with and in them.

The doctoral doors opened wider when Stephen Covey walked up to the lectern, soon becoming another change-maker in Norm's life. As a not-yet-famous author of the bestselling book, *The Seven Habits of Highly Successful People*, Covey gave Norm exposure to new ideas on management in his lectures that wouldn't be available to the general public for years to come.

> *Norm:* Stephen Covey set the stage for a discussion of principles of management that led to my understanding of strategic planning. What was most helpful was the way Covey cast these habits as a modern *modus operandi* to throw out or render obsolete most concepts of old, hierarchical management styles.
>
> Covey values *values.* He values people. He values people who are different. He values himself, his family, his coworkers. He values the spiritual, where most either sublimate it or wish it would go away.
>
> Covey taught us how values impacted the bottom line of institutions, like colleges, churches, schools, hospitals, and families. And that values help us decide what it is that really matters, whether in the work place or in our own lives. As we live in times of dramatic change that sometimes comes from unexpected directions, we must first listen to understand and then to be understood. When a myriad of variables is changing and intersecting, it's not surprising that we need to develop new "habits."

Norm's doctoral thesis assessed the evolving attitudes of American Lutheran Church members and clergy toward church colleges at a time of decreasing fiscal support and secularization of societal norms. He found most members were middle class citizens with moderate to conservative values, and while the majority were supportive of church colleges, it was the younger members who were most open to change. After receiving his degree in philosophy in 1972, he returned to ALC headquarters eager to apply what he had learned.

BE A LIGHT, NOT A JUDGE. BE A MODEL, NOT A CRITIC.
—STEPHEN COVEY

LEADERSHIP BEYOND ACADEMIA

At the same time Norm earned his doctorate, a new best seller caught his attention as it hit the bookstands. *Born to Win: Transactional Analysis with Gestalt Experiments,* authored by Muriel James and Dorothy Jongeward, heightened his awareness of the growing interconnectivity of the world. What he read not only validated his belief in the importance of individualism, it also broadened his understanding of the emerging need for developing leaders with a global mindset.

In his files, he kept a four-page handout of key excerpts from Chapter One in the book, entitled "Winners and Losers." A summary demonstrates the synergy between the views of the authors and my father (if this were written today, a "winner" would be a "leader," and masculine pronouns would be gender neutral):

> *Each human being is born as something new, something that never existed before. Each person can see, hear, touch, taste, and think for himself. Each has his own unique potentials—capabilities and limitations. Each can be a significant, thinking, aware, and creatively productive person in his own right—a winner.*
>
> *A winner is not afraid to do his own thinking or to use his own knowledge. He can separate facts from opinion and*

doesn't pretend to have all the answers. He's his own boss and knows it.

A winner cares about the world and its peoples. He is compassionate and committed to improving the quality of life. Even in the face of national and international adversity, he does not see himself as totally powerless. He does what he can to make the world a better place.

A GLOBAL VIEW: PEACE EDUCATION

In 1973, Norm and Jo accompanied ALC colleague Loren Halverson on a trip through Germany and Switzerland. A seed was sown as my father witnessed the effects of embedding peace into higher education curriculum. This visionary insight resembled his own father's early adoption of hybrid seed corn back in the 1930s.

> *Norm:* Halverson was helping rebuild Germany through *Kirchentag*, a grass roots lay movement mobilizing human resources for peace and social responsibility. From our experience accompanying him and attending a five-day peace initiative, it became clear that peace education could be a new way of looking at the whole purpose of church-led higher education. It was also clear that peace education embodied everything we had tried to express in the concept of a caring community. We began developing an educational strategy for preparing young people to learn "the things that make the peace."

On one last stop before heading home, Norm and Jo attended a World Council of the Church convention in Switzerland. Jo tells an amusing story about my father's well deserved "everyday man" reputation.

> *Jo:* At the conclusion of our dinner with members and spouses of the World Council of the Church, there was a back-up in the kitchen, and the servers were slow to clear

the table. Norm stood up, picked up some of the plates and brought them into the kitchen. He caused quite a stir, shocking those at the table as they explained that men didn't go into the kitchen. He must have left quite an impression.

Expanding to a global vision put wind in Norm's sails. He returned from Germany with a new red VW bug and a hunger to weave peace into the higher education curriculum. Back in the office, he was about to learn that big ideas come with a price tag. When the ALC announced a $20 million fundraising goal, he got a crash course in raising money, and off he went to convince others to invest. He made his pitch at a kickoff speech given at the Lutheran Educational Conference of North America in Seattle.

Norm: Twenty million dollars is not a lot of money for a church of two and a half million members. Do a little arithmetic and see what I mean. But $20 million is a lot of money for the colleges, seminaries, and campus ministry that will benefit from it. It will give them a boost larger than any single boost ever given by the Church. It's exciting and thrilling.

We cannot sit still and watch the world go by; therefore our church has launched the Lutheran Ingathering for Education (LIFE), not to build institutions but to enable young men and women to be planted and rooted in the world of which you are a part—*to be watered by love, justice, and mercy,* nourished by the solar power that God sheds on his people. We are building places on university campuses where students may gather and try to find meaning, and then scatter afar to sow new seeds in the world.

What Norm learned about raising money would carry over to record-setting results in the next chapter of his life. I learned, seemingly by osmosis, from what he was doing, modeling that helping others and doing it well is a joyous experience for the giver, receiver, and the matchmaker. This altruistic spirit is something we would eventually have in common as my career was shaped along this same approach.

JOB OFFERS AND THE FUTURE

He loved his work and turned down many job offers before one came along that was just too tempting to decline. Opportunity once again came knocking and a door was poised to open before him. On the other side would be his lifelong mission's fulfillment, the driving force he'd been true to all along: shaping young minds to think independently for leadership not only of this nation, but of the world.

> *Norm:* Very early, I had been asked to take a presidency at both Dana College and California Lutheran University. I had the sense that I wasn't ready. Once you're in, it's difficult to get yourself out, something that happens to people who want a job too much. Then in 1975, with Roanoke College... I don't know. The time was right. Everything lined up.

Our city life in beloved Minneapolis came to an end in 1975. Peggy went off to St. Olaf College, and Bill followed my father's footsteps to Wartburg, leaving me at home in Minneapolis for my senior year at South High. My world was about to pivot, and I would fiercely resist walking through the same door that had opened to my parents.

But Spirit had other plans in mind, and we moved to the place where my father was meant to be: in the heart of a small college campus, nestled in the foothills of the mountains, where he and Jo would connect deeply with students on a personal and life-changing way.

NORM'S LIFE LESSON #30

WHEN YOU WALK THROUGH AN OPEN DOOR, DON'T LOOK BACK.
"YOU CAN'T DRIVE A CAR BY USING THE REARVIEW MIRROR."

QUESTIONS FOR SELF-REFLECTION

- You've read about how Norm began to think more universally. For him a global vision was life changing. What is your world view and how did it develop? Why do you think it is important to understand the interconnectivity of the world?
- Are there writers or thought leaders who have influenced you? Do you seek enough opportunities to learn? If not, what holds you back?
- In a world of competing and often biased news sources, how can you keep your mind open to all sides and opinions? Do you seek out a variety of sources, some that even challenge your opinions?
- What are ways you can develop your skill set at work? If you aren't doing it, what might motivate you to start?

PHOTO TIMELINE

1935 Norm with his sisters going to school in Nebraska. Even at age ten, he was cognizant of racism.

1941 At sixteen, Norm (front) committed his life to serving others. His Deshler High football coach would be a key influence later in my father's life.

July 4, 1946 Norm (seated) and his father with the airplane won in a raffle at the age of twenty-one.

1951 In a ten-minute decision on the day he graduated from Wartburg College, Norm decided not to go to seminary and instead work as the Director of Public Relations for his alma mater.

1952 Norm met Jo on a blind date and fell in love with a stunningly beautiful career woman far ahead of her times.

1952 Jo always dressed to the nines, and (not ironically) red was her favorite color.

June 30, 1953 When Norm and Jo married, the committed to an equal partnership lasting a lifetime. Pictured here, they enjoy a modest honeymoon stopover on their way to Niagara Falls.

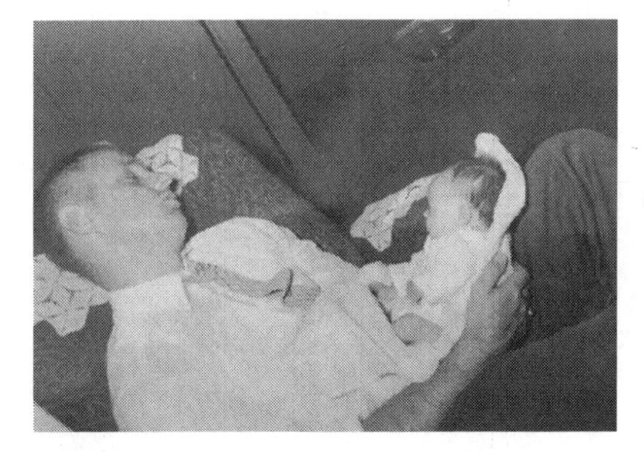

1959 Running on fumes, with three children in diapers, one with colic, Norm earned a Master's degree at the University of Wisconsin. Racism and equality were the topics of his research.

1959 My father carried this photo in his wallet until the day he died. It shows me, my mother, Bill and Peggy, when we lived in University of Wisconsin graduate school housing.

1960 A big move from a small-town Iowa to Golden Valley, an idyllic suburb of the metropolis of Minneapolis.

1967 My parents taught me to follow my own path and to question the rules. I tested this out by not worrying about earning the most Girl Scout badges.

1966 Norm boldly moved our family from the suburbs to inner-city Minneapolis, placing us in the heart of an integrated neighborhood. Peggy, Bill, and I (right) were 10, 9, and 8. In seventh grade, Jo sent me to school in pants, which led to the school to changing the dress code.

1968 While on a road trip to the Deep South, we happened to drive through Memphis when Martin Luther King Jr. was assassinated. In Louisiana, my father refused to enter "whites only" laundromats or churches, instead taking us where blacks were allowed.

1968 Norm and Jo bought an as-is cabin, complete with an outhouse, on Sand Lake, Minnesota, two hours north of the city.

1968 I wrote letters to my father, who commuted to the cabin on the weekends.

1968 Peggy, Bill, and I, along with our Sand Lake friends, sit on our red row boat, not knowing it would later become part of my life story.

1975 Dr. Norm Fintel became president of Roanoke College, three years after completing his Ph.D. in Higher Education. Our family is shown here, with dad seated at his desk, and his parents to the right. *(photo courtesy of Roanoke College).*

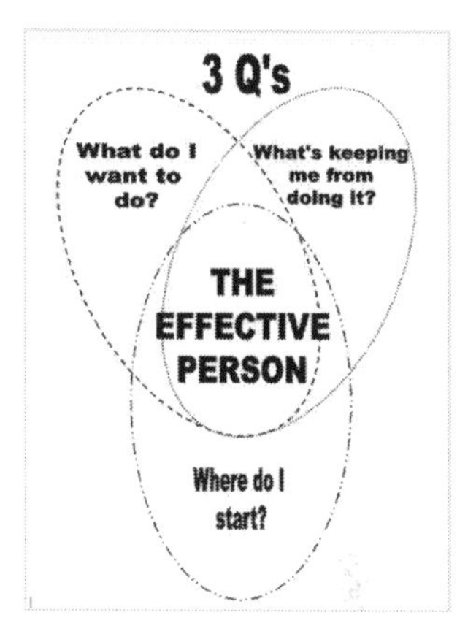

1975 Norm brought his "Three-Question" approach to developing personal and organizational effectiveness to his work at the college. His theories would become the basis for his book on leadership. To this day, I use this approach in my life and in my work with Dining for Women.

1980 As always, and especially during his tenure as president, Norm kept modeling the way forward to true equality. His open-door policy to four black students recruited for basketball was influential on all of their lives. Shown here are four players, known affectionately as the "Four Horsemen." *(photo courtesy of Roanoke College)*

1989 Norm retired from Roanoke College, and the Fintel Library was named in my parents' honor. *(photo courtesy of Roanoke College)*

1990's Norm and Jo focused on family, gathering every year for Thanksgiving on Sanibel Island, Florida.

1998–1999 Norm with Pastor Anna, who initially invited my parents to Tanzania.

1998–1999 Norm worked with church leaders, here with the Lutheran Bishop.

1998–1999 Norm advising at the Lutheran Agape School in Tanzania.

1998 Similar to my move to the inner city at age eight, when Nora and Jeanette were ten and eight, we took them out of school to visit Africa. My daughters (with their grandmother in the doorway), met students at an elementary school in Moshi, Tanzania.

The fact that I chose to take my daughters to Africa over summer break, instead of on a "traditional" American vacation, did not occur to me until I chose to include this photo in this book.

2002 Norm's first book on leadership, written for Lutheran leaders in Tanzania, is published. The title—*VIMIPUGOA*—is an acronym for vision, mission, purposes, goals, and actions.

2004 Norm's second book, *Effective Leadership*, is published for American audiences.

2003 Dining for Women is born. One of DFW's early grantees was Matrichaya, whose main objective is to provide education, self-employment, and healthcare to the under-privileged children and women in Ranchi, India.

2007–2012 Norm and Jo sold their cabin on Sand Lake in Minnesota and moved to Greenville, South Carolina to be closer to family. Norm began writing life lessons to his grandchildren. These lessons became the origination of this book.

May 2010 Norm and Jo at the wedding of their granddaughter, Leslie.

2013 Norm and Jo returned "home" to the Roanoke Valley, living close to Roanoke College at Brandon Oaks Retirement Community. Here, they stand on campus in front of the Fintel Library, named in their honor. *(photo courtesy of Roanoke College)*

2016 After I co-founded Dining for Women in 2003, our organization partnered with the Peace Corps as well as Michelle Obama's Let Girls Learn initiative, to take down barriers and send 62 million girls to school. (Left to right: Beth Ellen Holimon, DFW president; Michelle Obama; Marsha Wallace, DFW co-founder, and myself; *photo courtesy of Barack Obama Presidential Library)*

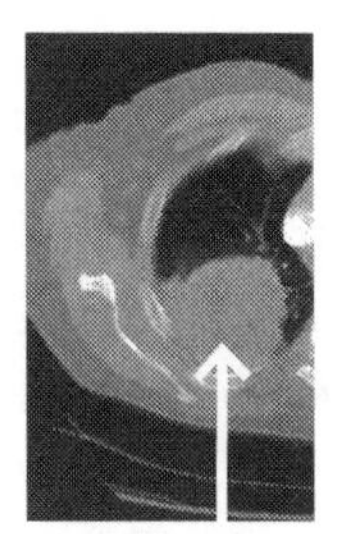

Tumor in lung before treatment

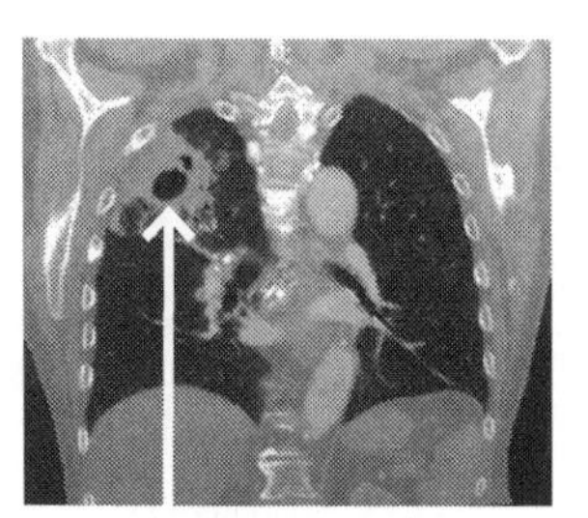

Hole in tumor after treatment

May 2016 Immunotherapy and sheer will sparked Norm's nine-month miracle remission. The literal hole in his tumor figuratively opened the door to the time he needed to leave his message of hope for the world.

2017 Norm with the statue of Martin Luther—a beloved and strong influence on my father's life—on the campus of Roanoke College.

2017 New life—Emma Stokes, Peggy's first granddaughter and Norm and Jo's fourth great-grandchild.

April 7, 2017 Norman D. Fintel, Ph.D., retired President of Roanoke College, passed away at 7:30am, at the age of ninety-two.

April 7, 2017 Jo and Norm had previously asked our family to attend the Roanoke College Medal Award Ceremony during Alumni Weekend. Norm died four hours before it started. Walking into the ceremony, we were greeted by Coach Ed Green (far left), Kenny Belton (third from left), along with two basketball team members and the Four Horsemen, who had all flown to Roanoke specifically to surprise Norm and Jo for the event. Jo asked Kenny to sit in my father's place at our table. *(photo courtesy of Roanoke College)*

April 7, 2017 LOVE fireworks celebration on campus during Roanoke College's 175th Anniversary Alumni Weekend—coincidentally the same day Norm died. *(photo courtesy of Roanoke College)*

2017–2018 More spirit sightings—Norm's favorite red geraniums surge in bloom on my deck after they had shriveled and died from my neglect.

2018 Dining for Women's 15th Anniversary Conference in May at the United States Institute of Peace, at the invitation of USIP president Nancy Lindborg, to share knowledge and collaborate with 300 Dining for Women members in attendance. *(photo courtesy of Dining for Women)*

August 30, 2018 Jeanette "Jo" Esther Kosbau Fintel passed away. I spent what turned out to be my mother's last three days of life reading the final draft of this book to her while she squeezed my hand in the parts she loved the most. Still holding hands, she died ten minutes after I finished reading the last page. I can only imagine she was anxious to go tell Norm all about it.

CHAPTER 11

Buds and Blossoms

SERVANT LEADERSHIP IN ACTION (1975–1978)

THE ONLY TRULY VIABLE INSTITUTIONS WILL BE THOSE THAT ARE PREDOMINANTLY SERVANT-LED.
—ROBERT K. GREENLEAF

ALL ROADS CONVERGED WHEN NORM WAS HANDED THE KEYS TO ROANOKE COLLEGE. He would bring his wisdom and values to the campus in the form of a quiet, level-headed, forward thinking man. Confident that he was in the right place at the right time as the college's new president, he would methodically set about shaping the minds and hearts of thousands of students.

Norm's integrity enveloped the college at a time when the nation was recovering from the remnants of the Vietnam War and the shocking scandal of Watergate, events that evoked a cynicism that rivaled our political climate of today. During this time of liberated social conventions, Norm brought a steady hand to the college community.

With Peggy and Bill in college, and plans for me to be enrolled at a high school down the street from campus, Norm and Jo could look forward to the luxury of extra time. They took a team approach to the new position and together nurtured a culture of open, authentic leadership.

During these years I observed my father's servant-based leadership style, unaware I was being introduced to my own calling, which, in later years, would flourish under his wise and exemplary mentorship.

CALL TO ROANOKE COLLEGE

Armed with his new Ph.D. from the University of Minnesota, and the accumulated knowledge of all his years shepherding colleges to thrive and adapt in an ever-changing world, Norm packed up his suitcase of values. This humble midwestern farmer headed off to Virginia to begin a new career as college president. Norm tells of what motivated him at that time:

> *Norm:* The idea of forging new paths to leadership is woven into the attraction of the two clarion calls which brought me to Roanoke College. One call was a commitment to values, and the second was to test whether the emerging principles of management and leadership I had found in my study of other colleges could be used to strengthen Roanoke's will for itself and its will to live for others.
>
> There was a challenge in America to restructure education. To me, this meant getting back to the values of honesty, integrity, trustworthiness, openness, and love. We needed this kind of moral persuasion once more; then, beyond that lay the surrounding community and then the whole world community.

Both Jo and Norm tell how events unfolded:

Jo: In April of '75, we flew from Minneapolis to Roanoke. The azaleas and the rhododendron were blooming in Virginia, while back home, Minnesota was still experiencing winter. In a private dining room in the basement of Hotel Roanoke, the college search committee sat around a long, oval table with us. I was introduced to peanut soup, and my queasy stomach wasn't sitting too well while they were asking both of us a barrage of questions.

Norm: We didn't hear from them, and by August I had thrown away all my Roanoke materials. Then the call came asking me to return (though Jo had apparently passed the test the first time and didn't need to return), so I went back on my own. I left one day on a 5 a.m. flight and was back in Minnesota at 2 a.m. the following morning with a job offer.

I accepted, and Jo and I agreed we would first be true to ourselves and operate in this new arena as a team. Jo's years at Roanoke brought out all her best qualities. Perhaps her finest trait was that of friendship with nearly everyone whose life intersected with her own. People sensed her genuineness and respond with undying loyalty.

For the next fourteen years, it was like an equally shared love affair—Roanoke had decided on us, and we'd decided on Roanoke.

AN UNFAMILIAR CULTURE

Coming in the middle of my senior year of high school, this move to Virginia was a painful one for me—not just because I'd be leaving my life and friends behind, but because I'd be entering a completely unfamiliar culture at a time in life when I wanted things to stay the same

I found out we were moving in late August, during the time my parents and I were spending the summer at our cabin on Sand

Lake. My father asked me to join him in our rowboat, which he motored to the middle of the lake, cutting the engine so we drifted the way of the wind, waves lapping gently at the boat's sides. He wanted to give the life-changing news he was about to impart the respect it deserved. In such an intimate setting of concern for what it would mean to me, a teenager in her last year of high school, he told me of their decision to accept the new job at Roanoke. I took it all in, but like the call of the loon, so prevalent on the lake, to me it all sounded like madness.

He had never, ever, told me what to do, but now what had been my long leash of freedom felt like a choke collar. I knew I would have to go, yet I did my best to find an alternative arrangement. My English teacher, Mary Michael Connelly, offered up her guest bedroom. But it was not to be. Dad put his foot down. Off to Virginia and a foreign culture I went.

While my parents were busy in their new lives, I was left with lots of freedom to find my bearings. I was naïve to assume that my inner-city school culture would be easily transplanted in the Southeast. Walking into Andrew Lewis High School on my first day, wearing my best green Levi corduroys and a silky shirt nicely tucked in, I was shocked to see all the girls wearing dresses. I thought we'd rattled that cage back in junior high, but here I was on a new playing field, once again.

The students were welcoming and forgiving of my different ways, but I can't imagine my "Yankee views" didn't raise a few eyebrows. I had to wonder what my teacher really thought when I turned in an essay praising the leadership of Democrat Hubert Humphrey.

Sensitive to my predicament, my father later in life asked me, "Did we do the right thing?" I told him, yes. The move forced me to adapt and be resilient. Despite giving my parents the silent treatment for at least three months, I grew and added speed to my fearlessness, though I needed to get hold of a tendency for reckless driving. My father was always, at every turn, patient with me, and he always knew when to step in when I was struggling. He did this not by telling me what to do but by being available at the exact moments when I needed a dose of unconditional love. He didn't have to say a thing; his presence was all it took. In these moments, his spirit joined mine and strengthened me.

VISION OF THE PRESIDENT

My father's vision for the college was simple, bold, and crystal clear.

> *Norm:* I wanted Roanoke to be the best liberal arts college it could possibly be. I was committed to educating the whole person. We wanted to be a college where quality is part of our very being. For me as president, Roanoke meant a relentless dedication to the pursuit of quality—to demand the best from all those around me and to demand that same quality of myself.

All of the values and knowledge planted and nourished in Norm's lifetime came into full bloom during his fourteen years at Roanoke. That culmination of wisdom is clearly present in the visionary message of his inaugural address, a speech that was frequently quoted over the time of his presidency. His words are excerpted here:

> ***THE VALLEY WAITS: PATHS TO LEADERSHIP***
>
> *We live in a world-wide valley, where our ideas and acts have an impact on the global society to which we belong. As a nation, as a world, but more importantly as individuals, we must be about the business of providing the opportunities and the environment for leadership to develop.*
>
> *The image of a rich and fertile valley waiting to be discovered, explored, and developed carries with it an air of expectancy, an air of awe and wonder that is needed to help us to be optimistic in a time when the heights confronting us*

seem almost unscalable. Where is the ethical and moral fiber in our society that would have made Watergate impossible, if not unthinkable?

Students need to be taught that one person can make an impact. Education should not have feet of clay. We must educate the whole student in the following four areas, for such a person will be a fruitful gardener in all the valleys of his or her life.

Intellectual—*to gain extensive knowledge in a field of study and problem-solving abilities*

Emotional—*to know oneself, to be sensitive to the needs of others, and develop ways of knowing one's own strengths and weaknesses*

Spiritual—*to develop a dimension concerned with values, morality, and ethics*

Practical—*to learn how to earn a living as well as how to live*

I am committed to being a servant leader, one who is a leader because he is servant to a cause and people that is larger than himself.

I am committed to a theme I call "paths to leadership"—a call for all of us to become all we can become for the sake of others.

The valley surrounding us waits to see what Roanoke College will do to use her wisely and with loving care.

THERE ARE ONLY TWO LASTING BEQUESTS WE CAN HOPE TO GIVE OUR CHILDREN. ONE OF THESE IS ROOTS, THE OTHER WINGS.
—JOHANN WOLFGANG VON GOETHE

INVITATION TO THE COMMUNITY

The "valley" referred to in his inaugural address was not only a metaphor for the world he hoped to impact in his new role, but quite literally, the geographical area in which Roanoke College was situated. During the fourteen years of his presidency, my father expanded the boundaries of the college to include the outside community—the Roanoke Valley and beyond. This was an important choice he made, and he went about it with his characteristic strategic planning, as described in his own words:

> *Norm:* Every community or organization has a small group (5-7) of people who are the power people. Look around you and your community, your church, your club. If you can be objective, you will have to admit that a few people are pivotal to all major decision-making.
>
> After a short while of asking people to name the leaders in the surrounding Roanoke Valley, I saw several emerge as the real change makers—all existing behind the scenes, none of them in positions of power, except they were.
>
> One day, I was talking with Jo about how hard it was to get the Roanoke city leadership, which was six miles away from the smaller sister city of Salem where the college is located, to think of Roanoke College as part of their domain. Sharing her insight, she came up with the little slogan, *It's a lot farther from Roanoke to Salem than it is from Salem to Roanoke*, meaning the college had kept itself isolated from the community and seemed a far-off destination to most in the town.
>
> I started thinking Jo's way, saying to myself, yes, that's because we haven't brought the greater community onto our college campus. So one of the first things we did when we got a little money was to put the Henry Fowler lecture series together (named for the former Secretary of State and Roanoke College alumnus) and make it free to all the

people. The first speaker was Henry Kissinger, and 6,000 people showed up. Then came President Jimmy Carter, Liz Taylor, and Lady Bird Johnson.

We began adding members to the Board of Trustees who were endowed with *sapiential authority*, which is authority that derives from wisdom more than from position or money. It was the power of ideas, of rightness, of character, that gave such leaders their authority. When we combined this ingredient with position and with a liberal use of financial resources, it is no wonder we were able to accomplish all that we did.

A NEW STYLE OF LEADERSHIP

An organization's mission acts as the beacon to unify everyone's work, whether it's at a college, a corporate office, or a non-profit. Norm knew that if you want everyone to row in one direction, it's not only essential to have a common mission—it's equally essential that everyone fully owns it.

> *Norm:* Thriving institutions share a common purpose, an unseen linking system which gives us corporate definition, the mission statement. If we can agree on the simplest, most basic premise, it brings us together around a common understanding of how we can best work together to accomplish our mission.

The current Roanoke College mission statement, which sounds like it came right out of Norm's inaugural address, reads like this: *Roanoke College develops students as whole persons and prepares them for responsible lives of learning, service, and leadership by promoting their intellectual, ethical, spiritual and personal growth.*

WITHOUT A VISION, THE PEOPLE PERISH.
—PROVERBS 29:18

Following his many years of experience with leadership audits back at the ALC, Norm knew that the first step of his own leadership would require he check his ego as he stepped into this new role of "head honcho." Once in check, his leadership philosophies could be effectively put into action, and the college blossomed.

> *Norm:* The president is elevated to a status and treated with deference and respect. Unless the president is very careful, he or she could easily be convinced people are hanging on every word, and then develop what I call "president-itis."
>
> Egos are necessary in leadership, and their degree of strength will vary greatly from leader to leader. When the ego is solidly strong, the style of leadership matters less. I think that's because people learn to trust a strong leader and then do what is needed to get the job done. This can be true even if one leader is authoritarian and another more consensus-oriented.
>
> There are, of course, con artists who assume they are qualified to take on top leadership but haven't the depth nor skills to do it. They really do not understand what it takes and therefore cannot measure themselves against the task.
>
> The ego needs to be kept in check. There is need to build it up to the required level of self-confidence. As I heard once, "A person who becomes conceited and arrogant isn't big enough for the job." You need a big capacity to say *I don't know* when you don't, but you must do that as a leader.
>
> So how does one balance a healthy sense of identity with the pitfalls of ego blindness? A leader needs his or

her own sense of personal mission to have congruence with the larger organizational mission. And one must place the organization above individual needs.

YOU ARE NOT THE PRESIDENT; RATHER,
YOU HOLD THE OFFICE OF THE PRESIDENT.
—ADVICE GIVEN TO NORM
EARLY IN HIS CAREER

Checking your ego at the door and the art of being humble was a lesson I learned early when growing up, often demonstrated by my father's example. It's a value that I've watched in action within the leadership of the most successful nonprofit entities I've worked with. None demonstrate its importance, as well as the challenges of achieving it, better than Dining for Women, where over 700 extraordinary volunteer leaders work together in a highly engaged collaborative framework. Those able to put aside their ego and put the mission above all else are the most effective leaders.

My father knew that once people had their egos in check, good management begins with leadership.

Norm: Leadership has many components: knowledge, skill, and brainpower—though it's wisdom that is essential and propels us to the high road. Wisdom is not limited to the highly intelligent. It can cut across the intellectual dimension.

My leadership philosophy comes close to the ancient words of oriental wisdom by the philosopher Lao-Tzu, as recorded in the 17th chapter of the *Tao Te Ching*:

> A leader is best when he is neither seen nor heard;
> Not so good when he is adored and glorified;
> Worse when he is hated and despised.
> Fail to honor people, they will fail to honor you.
> But of a good leader, when his work is done,
> his aim fulfilled,
> The people will say, "We did this ourselves."

In an analogy he had used before, my father compared good leaders to the functioning of a gyroscope, not surprisingly an instrument used in airplane navigation.

> *Norm:* The gyroscope is a dynamic top that spins according to the laws of motion, always spinning in the same direction. The beauty of the gyroscope is that it is not perfect. It wobbles all over the place. You cannot at any moment say that you are on course, so you need to stay alert. You can, however, depend on the gyroscope to keep you moving in the right direction. It cannot read where the mountains and storms are, nor tell you how to land. Its job is to get you there in a relatively straight line. Your job is secure. All you need to do is adjust to the myriad of changes, all the while being true to your mission.
>
> The point is, don't panic! Just because the world around you seems to be falling apart, don't abandon your mission. Look at your predicament as navigating through a storm. Don't jettison the fuel to lighten the load. A captain who has confidence in the mission will inspire the crew through almost any hardship, and nothing builds that confidence more than practicing on doable assignments that tie into the mission.

MANAGEMENT IS DOING THINGS RIGHT.
LEADERSHIP IS DOING THE RIGHT THINGS.
—PETER DRUCKER

STRATEGIC PLANNING

With the mission as a beacon, Norm followed his father's example and envisioned bold steps to the future. Assembling a senior administrative team, he challenged them to plan for the college's 150-year Sesquicentennial Anniversary in 1992, seventeen years in the future. This was the college's first strategic plan, inspired by former mentor Loren Halverson's "enable them with my absence" philosophy, Norm gave them a long leash to figure it all out.

Norm: We began work on the 1992 Plan for Excellence at an off-campus retreat at Smith Mountain Lake. Ultimately, it went well, but we had to wrestle with the tendencies of all participants, including the president, to look to the president for pulling it together. This was when I remembered Loren Halverson's dictum, *I will enable you with my absence.*

I could see that each cabinet officer kept looking for me to decide on issues, so I left them for several hours with a request that they work it through. Some recall I napped, but when I returned, they had gotten their heads together, taken the list of twenty or so "things to celebrate in 1992," and put it into a workable format. Dean of Academics Gerald Gibson took the lead in developing the structure and ultimately keeping score on our achievements.

We left the list open-ended so that anyone could add additional items to "celebrate." The list grew to forty-two goals. The rest is history. In 1992, the college celebrated in great fashion with forty-one of the forty-two goals marked

> off as accomplished. Another big celebration was held a few years later when goal number forty-two—acquiring a chapter of the national honor society—Phi Beta Kappa—was achieved.
>
> I must add that initially, as with all change, the plan was met with a good deal of skepticism, not only by the faculty but also by the board which thought, in view of our history, that we were "out of our gourd" to expect that much. The board later scaled down the plan with a price tag of $25 million.

With forty-two lofty goals, it was inevitable that Norm would need to devote at least half his time to raising money. My mother was one of his secret weapons; people loved her. Another was Jack Hills, a youngster at thirty-six when my father hired him as the vice president of resource development. The three of them set about raising the $25 million. All three were masters at building deep, long-term relationships, many of which sustain the college even to this day.

Under Norm's watch, they raised the $25 million early and launched a new goal of $75 million, which would be exceeded by $11 million. At the same time, the $4.6 million endowment would rise to $23 million by the time Norm retired. It is said that he raised more than $14,000 a day over his fourteen years. Yet, despite this, his sense of frugality surfaced once in a while, as remarked by my mother in recalling those days.

> *Jo:* Jack, Norm, and I would travel in Florida on a limited budget. Norm thought every dollar we didn't spend was a dollar in the endowment fund, so we'd stay in these crummy little hotels. One morning when we came out of our rooms, Jack said, "I could see right through the sheets—they were that thin!" And there were bed bugs, too. We still laugh about it.

Fortunately, Jo had a knack for entertaining that served their strategy well. Her love of the underdog, straight talking, and keen sense of humor endeared her to everyone. She brought an openness and engaging personality, a spark of life, which complimented my father's reserved, quiet, stoic leadership.

> *Norm:* We spent fourteen years in the fast lane, traveling thousands of miles on behalf of the college, planning and hosting parties, dinners, and receptions for the two thousand or more people who visited our home annually. Jo's creativity, organization, and efficiency made her job look easy.

LIFE IN THE PRESIDENT'S HOME

Living in the 10,000-square-foot president's home wasn't always easy. It was like living in a fish bowl with a constant stream of workers—housekeeping, maintenance, food service, landscapers—and most nights filled with entertaining company.

I once asked Jo how it felt coming from poverty in her childhood to be living in a college president's home. She told me that her family had lived in a small, apartment-like home on the estate of a wealthy family. When she was in fifth grade and her father was in jail, she babysat for the wealthy family's two children. At every lunchtime, she would heat up a can of tomato or chicken noodle soup and split it three ways. She was never paid. "I guess they thought the soup was enough," she told me.

Less than a year after living in the President's House, I set out for Madison College (now James Madison University in Harrisonburg, Virginia). Then followed a period of me trying to find myself. As a sophomore, I moved back home to Minneapolis and finished my degree at the University of Minnesota. At the same time, my brother and sister were each married, and as grandchildren were born, both of them moved their families to the Roanoke Valley.

I came home each summer and gravitated to the alumni and resource development office. The staff put up with me, taking me under their wing, and I was happy working on any project they assigned me. Jack Hills was directly responsible for encouraging me to explore this field, and to this day, he's still a mentor in my work. What appealed to me about raising money was the powerful changes that were possible when finding a donor who shared the same vision for advancing ideas. Watching my father work some magic on campus, I learned that nothing was impossible.

Dick Phelan, the food service director, also put up with me and let me be on the catering team for events held at the President's House. This exposure to people of all kinds, as well as attending events on campus, made me a better communicator and judge of people.

And, of course, I learned through osmosis, watching my father put his management and leadership philosophies to work. Looking back, I tucked away what I was learning from him, valuable lessons that later became driving forces in my own vocational development.

CULTURE OF EXCELLENCE

Norm's Midwestern attitude—open, no pretense, approachable, the everyday man—showed up in many places. He quietly walked campus, eating lunch with students, listening and gathering opinions from them that later would shape his decisions.

Norm was well-known for arriving late for meetings. Everyone knew to be respectfully patient, that he was probably held up talking with a student.

One example sums up his unassuming, humble manner, told by Peter Dunklin, who was on campus observing Norm's leadership style and would later write about it. I share Peter's words found in summaries of his interviews with my father:

"One evening, Norm was showing me the new gym that was built when he was president. Norm, always the realist, trimmed an $8 million project down to a doable $4 million and got it built. As he was showing it to me, a security officer came up, asked us if we were with the conference and told us we would have to leave because he was closing up."

Norm smiled and said, "It's okay, I have a set of keys." The security guard looked at us with grave concern. Norm smiled and said, "We probably haven't met. My name is Norm Fintel." The look on the guard's face said it all—the recognition, respect, awe, and warm feelings expressed told me Norm was for real.

My mom had her own style of engaging others on a personal level. She is the kind of person that, after talking to her, you have no idea why you just shared your deepest feelings and opinions. She often ingratiated herself to the maintenance and landscape crews when she'd deliver hot, homemade apple dumplings to their office, never seeing color, age, gender, or status.

My father's hands-on, "everyday man" approach had the opposite effect one time, involving cleanliness standards. This story has a connection to a time in the mid-'50s, at the parochial school where Norm's father was a custodian. Remember that his father quietly re-cleaned floors after Norm and his brother-in-law did what Ernie considered a sub-par job, not meeting his standards of excellence. My mother tells the story:

> *Jo:* We inherited a housekeeper when we moved into the President's House. The home was her domain, and she loved being Queen Bee. Early on, when we first arrived, she walked into the kitchen one day to find Norm down on his hands and knees. He was scrubbing the floor, and said to her, "This is the way I want this floor cleaned." He had literally scraped the dirt from the corners of the room. It wasn't long after that our inherited housekeeper resigned.

Looking back, I'm not sure what the faculty thought of their new president. Norm wasn't a traditional academic. I wonder what they thought when one night, at a foreign language dinner honoring him and Jo, he took off his coat, and, resurrecting mechanical skills from his airplane pilot days, repaired Dr. Patricia Gathercole's dishwasher that had begun misbehaving.

He especially rattled the faculty when he boldly changed the date for the fall school term to begin before Labor Day. This was met with unified protest but proved to be prophetic, as today nearly all colleges start early. As my mother tells it:

> *Jo:* For hours, Norm spoke at a faculty meeting, firmly outlining his belief that the school term should begin in August, before Labor Day, not after. He told them this decision wasn't about them, it was for the benefit of the students, allowing more time for classes and learning.
>
> After that meeting, good friend and faculty member Dr. Lynn Eckman knocked on our door, telling Norm that he still had at least one friend on the faculty.

NORM'S LIFE LESSON #31

CHOOSE YOUR BATTLES.

QUESTIONS FOR SELF-REFLECTION

- In your work place, is there a mission statement? Do you observe how it is put into practice?
- Often times, a strategic plan is developed, and then put in a drawer and forgotten. Is there a strategic plan in place at your work? Would you say it is followed? What are examples of this?
- Leadership is vital for achieving goals. How would you describe the style of leadership in your company? If you are not that person, what about your own style? Do you ever hear an internal voice telling you to check your ego? Should you listen more?
- If you are a boss, do you empower your staff to make decisions, or do you give them orders? Which way would you want your boss to inspire your work?

CHAPTER 12

In Full Bloom

SHAPING STUDENTS, EXPANDING FAMILY (1978–1989)

THE FUNCTION OF EDUCATION IS TO TEACH ONE TO THINK INTENSIVELY AND TO THINK CRITICALLY. INTELLIGENCE PLUS CHARACTER—THAT IS THE GOAL OF TRUE EDUCATION.

—MARTIN LUTHER KING JR.

WITH HIS STRONG VALUES FOR LEADERSHIP AND MANAGEMENT NOW ROOTED IN THE COLLEGE'S MISSION and looking forward to the 1992 Sesquicentennial goals, Norm turned his attention to the students. It was also an incredibly fruitful time for his family. All three children would marry, Peggy and Bill right after graduating from Roanoke and Wartburg. Seeds of abundance were planted when all but two grandchildren would be born beginning in 1982, one each year all the way to 1990. So much to do, so little time.

The time period of the late '70s through the '80s was a post-war era when the economy flourished under a two-term president, a Hollywood actor named Ronald Reagan, until Black Monday when the stock market crashed in October of 1987. The world witnessed a nuclear meltdown at Chernobyl, and lost beloved Indian Prime Minister Indira Gandhi and cultural icon John Lennon, both assassinated. And while we celebrated the eradication of small pox, AIDS became a word added to the dictionary.

As advances in computers revolutionized the way we did business, and the Internet would soon bring the world to our fingertips, it became clear to Norm that his hope for impacting the next generation needed a radical shift in the college curriculum.

RESTORING VALUES AND SHAPING STUDENTS

At a time when secularism was on the rise, Norm took bold steps to instill values into the student experience. Once again, as three major branches of the Lutheran Church merged, creating the Evangelical Lutheran Church Association, he shook things up, this time revitalizing a dormant department of religion that had dwindled to one student.

Dr. Robert Benne, who Norm hired to bring the religion department back to life, credits my father for revitalizing the Lutheran heritage of the college. In Benne's book, *Keeping the Soul in Christian Higher Education: A History of Roanoke College*, he cites several important moves Norm made to strengthen that relationship. One was inviting the Virginia Lutheran Synod to relocate to the Roanoke campus. Another was in having the college pledge, in Benne's words, to "offer a value-laden education for the whole person, so that they might become responsible citizens."

In his book, Benne referenced Norm's actions to one of my father's favorite adages: *Don't talk about it, do it.* Or, as Norm's father had taught him many years prior, *Don't just stand there, do something*!

EDUCATING THE HEART IS A CRITICAL
COMPLEMENT TO EDUCATING THE MIND.
—STEPHEN COVEY

Norm was a leader in integrating rigorous academics with moral leadership development. He raised the academic bar in admissions by creating an Honor Society, then began the long process for achieving Phi Beta Kappa chapter status.

Not every decision was popular, and some remind me of a parent doing what is best for the child by keeping the child from harm's way. When he set in motion downgrading from Division II to Division III athletics, no doubt he rattled a lot of cages. This meant no more athletic scholarships. Norm wanted the money saved and re-directed to programs for improving the student's academic rigor.

In tandem with troubling national rising trends for recreational drinking and drug use, my father banned alcohol on campus, sending some shockwaves through campus dorms and fraternities.

NORM'S LIFE LESSON #32

DON'T LET THE BASTARDS GET YOU DOWN.
DON'T LET THEM SEE YOU SWEAT.

Engaging students on a personal level was important to my parents. Both Norm and Jo set about getting to know students on a first-name basis, listening, nurturing, and, as they did with everyone, looking inside to bring out the best in them. My sister Peggy understood this best, as she would transfer to Roanoke in her junior year and experience student life first hand. She also met Doug, another student, whom she would marry after graduating.

Being actively involved on a personal level was a team effort that created lifelong bonds between the college and its graduates. Propagating these bonds in the student years reaped benefits for garnering support from alumni for future endeavors of the college. A brilliant idea came from my mother and is a tradition still carried on today at Roanoke.

> *Jo:* An idea popped into my head for creating lasting bonds with the students after they graduate. While we continued the tradition of inviting all freshman to the president's home early in their first semester, grilling hot dogs and socializing, it occurred to me we needed to do something special for them in their senior year before they graduated. I wanted them to have a lifelong sense of belonging in the college community, so we bought wood burning tools and "sacrificed" the built-in shelving surrounding the large downstairs den where we gathered for a pre-graduation, sit-down steak dinner, inscribing names on it. Returning and searching for their names burned into the woodwork became an effective way to reconnect and sustain lasting friendships with our alumni.
>
> When the seniors were with us, we'd take them on a tour of the house, bringing them up to the third story rooftop to discover the answer to the long-held community rumor that a swimming pool sat on top of the President's Home. From street level, people could see what appeared to be a water slide, and because the rooftop area was so large, the rumor took hold that there was a pool on top of the house. At our senior dinners, students would discover the answer but were all sworn to secrecy in order to keep the rumor alive.

Before I knew about the "secret," I invited some high school friends over to the President's House when my parents were out of town. Word spread quickly, and our numbers swelled as students arrived to see for themselves whether or not there was a pool on the roof. I shudder to think what would have happened if social media had been invented back then.

Halfway through their tenure, in a bold move, Norm and Jo surprised everyone by moving out of the President's House to a much smaller residence next to the library in the heart of the campus, a decision reminiscent of their move from Golden Valley to the inner city. Again, they wanted to be where change was happening and live closer to the students on a daily basis.

> *Norm:* I wanted students to know that Jo and I were a part of their life here, that this is a community.
>
> Jo suggested it. She said, "Let's move." The smaller house was available. We had four more years until retirement. "Wouldn't it be fun to live on campus?"

> *Jo:* Because we moved, we got to know the class of '89 well. We retired at the same time as they graduated, and in an expression of friendship, they painted a large sign with the words *Not 14 years but a lifetime* and included a picture of us with grey hair. When we were traveling in New York, they put it in our front yard to surprise us when we returned. It was one of the highlights of our time with students.

My father was often spotted in the college commons, sharing a meal with students in the cafeteria, always listening and learning. Taking advantage of podium opportunities, he challenged students to examine their lives. The following excerpts from commencement speeches demonstrate his message, which is as pertinent today as it was forty years ago.

COMMENCEMENT SPEECHES AT ROANOKE

> *It's not so much a college's role to give students answers, as it is to help them ask the right questions, define the problems—to educate them for a responsible and thoughtful life.*

In a new age where interdependence is key, what values must we hold to enable us to live peaceably in one world? In many ways this is a serious, uninviting, volatile time to be graduating, when change not only can but does occur. It is a time when those prepared to step onto paths of leadership will find enormous challenges and rewards.

Each generation learns from the preceding, but still, each new generation is always left to cope with the "now" realities at its own time, pace, and speed.

My visits with you, my watching you perform in so many ways on campus, tells me you are on the way toward establishing your own competence and also conscience—a strong desire to do what is right and best. We need not one or the other but both. Leadership—in the home, in the office, in whatever job you have, in the community, state or nation—at any level demands competence, but leadership without conscience is demagoguery.

We can approach all of our learning and living experiences by asking questions.

Is it right? Is it true? Is it just? Is it fair for my neighbor?

What is the nature of the physical world in which we live and manage to keep it habitable?

What kind of living, biological creatures are we, and how do we relate to each other and to other forms of life?

What kind of social, cultural, and historical people are we?

What organizations and structures do we need to govern and rule ourselves?

And more personally: What kind of person am I? Who is my neighbor and what is he/she like?

I am optimistic about the future because men and women like you are going to be out there wrestling with the problems and opportunities of the 21st century and building toward a world of interdependence and peace.

If all college admissions could recruit students based on this commitment, enrollments would be overflowing.

Norm: I remember a joyful moment at commencement when a guy in the graduating class came up to me and said thanks for getting me to come to this college. For everyone who came and said something, you know there were ten, twenty, thirty more who would have if they had thought about it. But that was enough for me to keep on moving in the direction of trying to serve the world in which I lived, which was, in a sense, my vocation.

EQUALITY AND RELIGIOUS FREEDOM

This was a time in our nation's history when some big barriers turned into open doors, leading to a long, winding road toward peace and true equality with strides in gender equality. Margaret Thatcher was sworn in as the first female prime minister of England, and our nation took a day off, honoring Martin Luther King Jr. In 1981, Sandra Day O'Connor was unanimously nominated as the first women to wear the robes of the Supreme Court, and in 1983, astronaut Sally Ride was the first woman to launch into space.

Through it all, Norm kept modeling the way forward towards true equality. We begin to see an ever-widening portal of opportunity, taking him beyond the halls of academia and into minds and hearts on a local, national, and even global scale.

Jo: One of our first trips took us out West to meet alumni. I remember one, who happened to be white, asked Norm, "How many blacks do we have on campus now?" Norm replied, "Not enough." After that, Kenny Belton and five of the black basketball players came to campus, and we were so happy. They stole our hearts.

Norm didn't ask the dean of students to keep a watchful eye on the handful of African-American students that coach Ed Green had recruited for his team. He did it himself.

Five black basketball players had tentatively enrolled when the rest of the student body was white. With my father's 24/7 open door policy, a mentor relationship developed that would influence the trajectories of these five students' lives. Jo became their home-away-from-home mom. In the late '70s, the team didn't lose a game, won the conference, and team members were honored as campus leaders.

It wasn't until later, when Norm was diagnosed with cancer and in his last year of life, that we learned the power of his quiet, hands-on influence in their lives. Their stories of how Norm taught them how to navigate around obstacles, giving them confidence and resilience that would last a lifetime, will be shared in Chapter 12. First, we move on to his stance on religious tolerance.

> *Norm:* Sig Davidson was an alumnus and member of the board of trustees by the time Jo and I stepped onto the campus. Over the years, we got to know him well. I told Jo once that I thought of him as being the brother I never had. We talked a lot about Roanoke and his experiences as a former student on this putatively Lutheran college campus.
>
> We talked about religion at times. I resigned from the private Shenandoah Club when Sig, then a trustee of the college, was refused membership in the private social club because he was Jewish. I resigned because I'd observed a pattern of discrimination in membership selection—there were no black, Jewish, or women members. I was embarrassed. The college had Jewish board members, faculty, and students. I believed Roanoke should stand for the principle that all people have the inherent right of equality of opportunity.
>
> The controversy prompted numerous letters to the editor in the local paper, both decrying and defending the club. Vandals spray-painted Nazi swastikas outside the club's Franklin Road entrance.
>
> I tried to work within the system to change the admission policies of the club but felt staying in the club

> was no longer feasible. I don't dispute the right of a private club to choose its own members. It is simply my choice not to be part of it.
>
> The local paper reported that 150 Roanoke donors were members. While we thought some support might be lost, I sensed that most members would understand the reason and continue to support the college. It's a good club, and they're good people. As president of a liberal arts institution, I needed to support democratic principles, such as freedom and liberty, as well as the college's mission of nurturing a society where merit is the winning tool.
>
> The Shenandoah Club came to its senses shortly thereafter, and I returned. It is strange but true that our societies change very slowly and often for less than admirable reasons. Old ways that may have been in many ways good but are no longer, die hard.

Students weighed in through *The Brackety-Ack*, the weekly student newspaper, saying that while Fintel "didn't want to make a big deal of his resignation… they ran the story because students should see their president… is a principled person."

"I think it's a good thing for students to hear that he made a moral decision and a tough one," said Mike Taylor, then editor of *The Brackety-Ack.*

BE THE CHANGE YOU WANT TO SEE IN THE WORLD.
—MAHATMA GANDHI

FAMILY GAINS AND LOSSES

My siblings Peggy and Bill were both married in 1979, soon after graduating from college. Peggy and Doug Horn settled down in Roanoke, and after marrying Connie, his high school sweetheart,

Bill moved to Charlottesville for his oncology residency, eventually settling in Roanoke in 1988. Somehow, Bill and Connie managed to have their first three boys while he was in medical school and they were struggling to make ends meet.

Grandchildren didn't waste any time arriving. Earning the title of first born, Peggy's Julie arrived in 1982, and for the next eight years, eight more were born, one each year. Next came Leslie, Andrew, Stephen, Robert, Michael, Nora, David, and Jeanette.

I was still happily single after graduating from the University of Minnesota with a degree in gerontology, but I was forced to move back to my parents' home at Roanoke to recover from spinal injury that resulted from a roller-skating mishap. While recovering, I enrolled in a master's degree program at Virginia Tech when a door opened for me to manage Warm Hearth Village, a beautiful new retirement community in nearby Blacksburg. It was there that I fell in love with working in the nonprofit sector and start-up culture.

When the management company I worked for was replaced, I worked directly for the community's founder, Dr. Wybe Kroontje, before some unknown force called me back to Minnesota. I picked up and moved to Minneapolis without a job. Fearlessly, I set up informational interviews with resource development departments around the Twin Cities before finding a home at William Mitchell College of Law.

Like Norm in his first years at Wartburg, I simply loved my job. Starting as assistant director of the annual fund, I stepped into the position of director of alumni and resource development when there was a quick turnover. Being in over my head, I hired my mentor, Jack Hills, as a consultant. It was at this point that my father turned into my Yoda.

I was happily in the midst of a capital fund drive for the new law library when, returning from a work event, I met Greg, my future husband, in an airport in Winnipeg. My world turned upside down, and shockingly, we married within six months. I was 29, the same age as my parents when they married. Reluctantly, I left William Mitchell for Green Bay, Wisconsin, because Greg was a partner in an engineering firm and wasn't as transportable.

Right before moving, we lost my grandparents, my father's parents, in rapid succession. Norm didn't live with many regrets, though living far from his parents may have been one of them. Here is his story about losing them and the magic of their love:

> *Norm:* When I told my father about accepting the job at Roanoke, his response was, "That's too bad." Funny, I knew exactly what he was thinking: *Oh, you're going to be so far away.* It was hard to lose both of them within a short period of time, especially when we lived across the country.
>
> The twinkle in Ernie's eye whenever he was near Nora, my mother, didn't go unnoticed. Everyone knew they shared a special love connection. Even a disabling stroke, robbing him of clear speech and mobility, didn't hold him back from loving her with all his heart. It was shocking when she was the first to go.
>
> In the middle of one frigid, blizzardy March night, Ernie woke up to find Nora's side of the bed empty. Finding her slumped on the kitchen floor, he had to muster sheer strength of love and will to make his way across the street and pound on a neighbor's door for help.
>
> My mother died on Tuesday before Ash Wednesday. My dad died in a nursing home, forty days later on Easter morning. He was so much in love with my mother that many times I said if she went first, he would die within forty-eight hours. I was wrong. It was forty days. But I digress.
>
> I was at his side when he died, a sad day but even so, a day of rejoicing that he and my mom could be together again. They had lived out their lives according to their principles and pragmatically according to what was possible. Dad taught mostly by example, my mom by softness mingled with grit and an abounding love for all of us.

The next few days after his passing were blurry and sad but not unhappy sad. What came over me slowly was the realization that I was now the last generation the clan could turn to.

GLOBAL LENS—EAST-WEST GERMANY, RUSSIA, FINLAND 1988

As Norm entered his final years at Roanoke, he and Jo undertook a second trip to Germany that opened his eyes and helped him envision the world in the minds of students. He grasped the need to embed a global lens into the higher education curriculum.

It's important to understand context for the unbelievable timing and substance of this trip. With the world becoming increasingly interconnected, Norm returned to Germany a few years after President Ronald Reagan had signed legislation creating the bipartisan United States Institute of Peace in Washington, DC, an institution devoted to the nonviolent prevention of global conflict. Congressional leaders who lived through the devastation and destruction of war hoped to prevent more in the future.

Nothing makes sense about his trip except that the spirit opened this door and gave him a roadmap to advance his higher calling in life. Remarkably, I would find myself on the same roadmap years later, one that would lead me to the front door of the United States Institute of Peace for the 15th Anniversary Conference of Dining for Women in 2018. The USIP is a place where Norm would have experienced a bit of heaven on earth, their logo being, *Making Peace Possible.*

Let's remember that in 1961 the Communist government in East Germany had built a barbed wire and concrete wall to keep out Western "fascists," curbing the flow of massive emigration and defection to the West. The year before my parents visited Germany, President Reagan gave his most famous speech challenging Soviet leader Mikhail Gorbachev to "Tear down this wall!" The year after my parents visited Germany, on November 9, 1989, the wall was torn down, and the Cold War began to thaw, freeing citizens to once again cross the border. That night an ecstatic crowd from East and West, estimated at two million, swarmed the walls with hammers and picks, chipping it away.

On their trip before all this would happen, Jo recalls crossing from East to West Germany in a van. At the wall's security checkpoint, they were scrutinized, guards checking all documentation and using mirrors to look under the vehicle. She remembers what she called "drastically different moods" on each side of the wall.

Norm's actions upon return are described in an inspiring report presented to the college's board of trustees, a report that remains pertinent for those of us living in the world today.

> *Norm:* Our original purpose of spending three weeks in Germany, Russia, and Finland was to join Lutheran educational leaders and study East-West relations with an eye toward locating resources of people, places, and ideas for extending global awareness to our campuses and beyond. The idea of striving for world citizenship might be more descriptive of our agenda.
>
> We spoke with Marxists leaders. We visited the home of Martin Luther. We traveled to the Soviet Union where Mikhail Gorbachev was stating his vision for *Glasnost* or "openness" in government, a topic that was right up my alley. There is no substitute for talking to people of other cultures and participating in lectures, seminars, and programs to force one out of old thought patterns.
>
> Common to all people we talked with was the desire for upholding the real values necessary to any society—honesty, truthfulness, integrity. No government can long be effective without these values. One only needs to read our newspapers today for evidence.
>
> *What we learned:*
>
> - *Freedom is our greatest asset.*
> - *The East and West share many fundamental values.*

- *Free-enterprise and capitalism works better.*
- *Bureaucracy in any language spells problems.*
- *Peace is a fervent hope among the people of the world.*
- *Stoicism—resignation—suspension of belief masks their hope.*

There was a deep concern for peace, and we found this hunger for peace everywhere we went. It was clear we must develop a consciousness of global citizenship and teach others so that through better understanding of our world as one world, we will be able to expand peace and shrink warring capabilities.

Norm returned home with an agenda that would crescendo until the end of his life. I know he would have found a sense of inner peace had he known what I learned in May 2018, when my work took me to the United States Institute of Peace. In a conversation with two Minnesota-born USIP leaders—President Nancy Lindborg and Director of Gender Policy and Strategy Dr. Kathleen Kuenhast—I learned that an academic guide for peace and conflict resolution for higher education was made a reality in 2014.

Norm's anxiety over the state of the world evoked nightmares in his last days and ultimately gave impetus to him urging me to write this book. He would have loved knowing peace-building curricula was being implemented not only in higher education but also in elementary, middle, and high schools as a result of USIP's advancements.

NORM'S LIFE LESSON #33

PLANT THE SEED, WAIT FOR THE HARVEST.

LEAVING ROANOKE COLLEGE, 1989

By the end of my father's presidency, Peggy, Bill, and I were all married, and Norm and Jo had eight grandchildren. Greg and I were living in Green Bay, Wisconsin, with our daughter Nora, and I was happily employed in the development and alumni department at St. Norbert College.

Back at Roanoke, my father attended his final commencement ceremony, and after he spoke, the students in the graduating class of 1989—those they had gotten to know after moving onto campus—all rose to their feet and broke into a rehearsed song of tribute. His final remarks…

> *Norm:* There is the challenge in America today to restructure education… to get back to values of honesty, integrity, trustworthiness, openness, and love. We need this kind of moral suasion. Then beyond that lies the whole world community. If I had ten more years, I would tackle building world understanding, global consciousness, so that we would think of ourselves as world citizens. I want this college of mine—I will adopt it forever—to be a college that looks ahead to see what the challenges are.
>
> Be yourself, believe in yourself, look at life as an adventure, dare to dream, think only big thoughts, and always keep on learning. Give generously to those not as fortunate as you are.
>
> And, may your children all come to Roanoke College.

Before leaving campus, there was one more legacy yet to be bestowed, as told by my mother:

> *Jo:* When Norm made a special trip home from the office on one of our last days to tell me they wanted to name the new library after us, we both just sat there stunned. And we're still stunned. It was so totally unexpected and very humbling.

> There was to be an $8 million expansion and renovation of the 1961 library which was never named. Bowing to gentle pressure, we accepted the naming "in the spirit it was made." Norm had previously said he wouldn't consider having the library named after them. We finally agreed when an anonymous donor (a friend) gave $3 million and asked us to do so.

When Norm retired, he was asked why he thought he was so effective at Roanoke. Typical Norm, he replied, "I just acted out who I was." And when asked what he'd do next, he said, "I'll be on the lake in Minnesota. We'll watch the birds, mow the lawn, tend the garden, and watch the paint dry. The loons and ducks, and some fishing give us plenty to do. We have a telephone and a bathroom now, you know."

QUESTIONS FOR SELF-REFLECTION

- Norm made some bold decisions in his time at the college. What values did he bring to work which are the basis for these decisions?
- In your own work, are there examples of when your values influenced your decisions?
- What are some examples of Norm's work that stand out that you might want to emulate?
- When did you begin to form your own "global lens" through which to see the world? How does it compare to Norm's?
- Were you aware of the United States Institute of Peace? If not, take some time to get familiar and read some of their publications, available through their website at usip.org/publications

PART III

Harvest Season

1989–2017

CHAPTER 13

A Man for All Seasons

REAP WHAT YOU SOW
AND CELEBRATE
(1989–1997)

A MAN'S HARVEST IN LIFE WILL DEPEND ENTIRELY ON WHAT HE SOWS.
—GALATIANS 6:7

RETIRING FROM ROANOKE COLLEGE AFTER FOURTEEN YEARS, NORM COULD FINALLY BASK IN THE LUXURY OF PERSONAL TIME. Now he could spend more time with family and even put pen to paper to start writing a book to share his well-earned wisdom on value-driven leadership. Enjoying these pursuits, the Thinking Man was happy, but he would soon begin a new phase of service by once again heeding the call, this time stepping in as interim president for different colleges.

It was the '90s, and unfathomable violence by the Chinese government was shown on TV to take place on the streets of Tiananmen Square, leaving 100 to 5,000 protesters, many students, dead—depending on who was counting. American values were rocked with incidents of sexual harassment at work, and at the highest level with the impeachment of President Bill Clinton for fabricating the truth.

We began our love affair with a new device called a smartphone and added texting as an additional way to communicate. PlayStation and Nintendo became obsessions of our young people. Levity was welcomed into living rooms as our toddlers enjoyed Sesame Street's newest feature, *Tickle Me Elmo*.

Through all of this, comfort was found in the embrace of family, and Norm and Jo tightened those bonds on the beaches of Florida, at Sanibel Island on the Gulf of Mexico, gathering us all year after year for Thanksgiving. We begin with the day after Norm retired.

RETIREMENT... OR NOT!

On the day after he retired from Roanoke College, The River Foundation announced that Norm was taking on leadership of their work to develop Explore Park, a "living history" state park situated along the Roanoke River gorge. He was also serving on many local boards and chairing a $7 million campaign for the Salem YMCA.

My mother describes his life of retirement:

> *Jo:* He retired in 1989 at the age of sixty-four, having served Roanoke College for fourteen years and his church for thirty-eight. He didn't reach his goal of becoming president of the United States, but speaking as his wife, I'm glad he didn't.

My father's view on retiring:

Norm: I marvel at the world and its complex simplicity,

> its vastness and its availability to us. The curse of "work" seems to be that we lose sight of our personal vision and purpose. We have our moment on the stage and then we move on. As Robert Frost famously said, "Life goes on."
>
> Circumstances change, yet what is unchanging is the warp and woof of the Universe—that immense balancing act of energy and motion that produces our environment and life as we know it. One has only to look at the events in the world to know that something else is out there: Forces that would destroy rather than build. When seen in that light, there's "nothing new under the sun!" There is work to be done, and I'm ready for what is before me.

Over the next decade and into the 21st century, Norm's life looked less like retirement than it did a new chapter of active engagement in family, as well as leadership in extended academic settings. His continuous dedication to education and moral leadership required that he and Jo move frequently, always returning to the Roanoke Valley, to stay in touch with our growing family.

YOU CAN RETIRE FROM A JOB BUT DON'T EVER RETIRE FROM MAKING EXTREMELY MEANINGFUL CONTRIBUTIONS IN LIFE.
—STEPHEN COVEY

HOME AND FAMILY

Shortly after leaving Roanoke College, Norm and Jo settled into a home they built near campus in Salem, and with their future in mind, they added a suite of rooms on the ground level should they ever need a caretaker. It was a typically practical move, although over the next decade, their nomadic spirits would disrupt this plan. Soon after, they would break free from the "bondage" of home ownership and begin a game of musical homes.

My parents now turned their attention to their nine grandchildren. Getting to know them was the top priority. Their last two grandchildren, David and Jeanette, had arrived, and they enjoyed traveling to and from the homes of Peggy now in Atlanta, Bill in Pulaski, Virginia, and me in cheese head country, Green Bay, Wisconsin. Fortunately for my brother and sister, them living nearby meant their kids were exposed early to the beneficial influence of Norm and Jo.

One of my favorite stories of Norm and Jo's adjustment to retired life takes place soon after they moved into their new home in Salem. My father titled his writing about it "Dandelion Wine."

> *Norm:* Last Saturday, in the midst of my chores—washing windows and cleaning up—I was called to help Jo pick dandelions. She had read a recipe in the local paper, describing a recipe for dandelion wine.
>
> I spent the next half hour plucking those damned yellow heads. They stained my fingers and my pants as well, but nothing would do but to pick four quarts of the blessed sunshine flowers. I was spending nearly $200 a year on a lawn service that eradicates dandelions, so we had to go to a neighbor's yard to pick more of them.
>
> The recipe called for a crock and four gallons of boiling water to be poured over the mess with other ingredients such as yeast. That mess was soaked for a day, and then strained and allowed to ferment for four days before bottling and corking the liquid.
>
> Before bed that night, when I went to inspect the brew in the garage, I caught a yeasty odor. Every one of the bottles had blasted its cork, and the wine was dripping off my workbench onto my gas cans and other tools, all the way out the door. I refused to clean it up at that late hour, and Jo was already in bed, watching a mystery. I told her I had a mystery question for her, which was, How many of the bottles had blown their corks? Her response, "All of

them?" She must have had a premonition.

Next morning, we salvaged one bottle's worth of the brew. Jo put it into a couple of smaller vinegar bottles with metal spring caps. She worried that even so, the bottles might shatter, so she put a plastic grocery bag around them, thinking it might hold the shards. I hoped that if there was an explosion, it wouldn't damage the cars or spray the ceiling.

Norm didn't have to repaint the garage ceiling, as the bottles survived, only to be consumed at a dinner party by a few brave friends.

Apart from living in Salem, Norm and Jo made the Minnesota cabin at Sand Lake home every June through August, the only months guaranteed to be warm enough for comfort. Between the years 1989-2004, Sand Lake was a gathering place for family and friends. In the winters, as much as possible, they headed south to the Gulf Shore, making "snow bird" friends wherever they went.

I was the only one living close enough to spend considerable time at Sand Lake. After my daughters Nora and Jeanette were born, Greg and I bought the rustic cabin (tiny, no heat, lots of blown fuses if you plugged in two electrical appliances at the same time) next door to my parents, reasoning that the six-hour commute was worth the opportunity for grandparent influence in our daughters' early development. Indeed, this proved true, as my parents were able to have a life-long influence on them both.

Jeanette followed Grandpa everywhere, to the gravel pit on a hunt for agates and up a tall ladder when the cabin needed new paint. Once, when she was 4 or 5, I saw her racing down the path to our cabin, carrying her fishing pole with Grandpa chasing after her. It turned out she was protecting the worm on her hook when Grandpa needed to cut the fishing line. She loved all creatures and would secretly help fish intended for the dinner table escape from the stringer.

Once every summer, we'd all ride the ten miles along the bike trail to and from Willow River for breakfast at a diner called Peggy Sue's. It was on one of these long bike rides that Nora rattled my father with the question, "Grandpa, do you know everything?" This tripped a humility trigger that he revisited many times over the rest of his years.

NORM'S LIFE LESSON #34

CHECK YOUR EGO, EVEN WHEN YOU HAVE ACCUMULATED DECADES OF SAPIENT WISDOM.

These summers with their grandparents had lasting influence in the lives of both my daughters. You can hear some of them in this school essay Nora wrote when she was 12 or 13. Nora was named after my father's mom, as well as for her grandfather (Norm).

WHERE I STAND, BY NORA COLLINS

I believe that everyone should be treated the same, even if they are a different race. I believe that everyone should get a good education. I believe that peace is always better than war. I believe that people can do anything if they set their mind to it.

I don't care for any sort of reptiles. I do not care for terrorists or kidnappers. I really do not care for creepy, crawly, insects in my home. I do not care for violent movies. I do not care for selfish people. I don't care for negative attitudes toward life. And I really don't care for people who make other people feel bad.

I'm tired of hearing about all the innocent people dying in the world. I am tired of hearing about all the terrorist attacks. I am tired of hearing about all the innocent kids getting kidnapped. I'm really tired of all the pop stars turning into movie stars. I am also tired of hearing about all the money football players get paid, and they still want more.

I prefer positive attitudes to negative attitudes. I prefer comedy movies to violent movies. I prefer AOL to Yahoo, and fruit to vegetables. I prefer afternoon to the morning. I also prefer the sunset to the sunrise.

It was during this time that physical trauma upended my life, testing my resilience. I first experienced back pain in high school gymnastics, which then progressed until a roller-skating fall made it a permanent condition in my life. Three spinal surgeries in seven months left me disabled. Surgical error first left a pedicle screw pressing on my central nervous system, and its early removal led to another breaking off in my vertebrae. The eleven hours to remove the broken screw left me with chronic pain, forcing radical changes in every aspect of my life.

No longer able to work in a traditional setting, I wrestled with how to pivot, and eventually I waded back by serving on a local YWCA board and shifting from working in higher education development to consulting for a variety of local non-profits. I found my passion for grassroots non-profits and was set on the path for co-founding and shaping my own organization. During this time, Norm continued to be my Yoda, as we put our heads together on several consulting projects.

A NEW CHAPTER: INTERIM PRESIDENCIES

As they moved north and south with the seasons, my parents would experience the phone ringing with multiple requests from colleges for Norm to serve in an interim role during the college's search for a new president. He accepted some of these requests, namely, to come on board for colleges in California, Illinois, and Texas, and in 1990, he and Jo were on the move again.

Serving only in short term roles, Norm, you'd think, would have time for status quo and stability. But "status quo" wasn't a word in my father's vocabulary. As he learned in graduate school, there was "nothing new under the sun." He'd quickly find areas of weakness at the administrative and leadership levels, and set about turning them into strengths.

This was a time when the nation was reeling from a devastating school shooting that left thirteen dead at Columbine, Colorado, and the issues of bullying and gun control had become a national agenda. Norm took advantage of opportunities in his interim roles, challenging young people to rise up and lead. At California Lutheran University, he called on students to help bring out the best in our nation.

California Lutheran was where Norm met Peter Dunkel who, at 29, was a rising star working in the college's development office. Norm saw potential and encouraged Peter to pursue a doctoral degree, becoming Peter's mentor as well as the subject of Peter's doctoral research on leadership. They energized one another so much that they decided to co-author a book on leadership. Just before the book's publication, Peter died suddenly at the age of thirty-four, devastating my father. It would take another eight years for Norm to complete the book they had started together, *Effective Leadership: A Guide for Church and Nonprofit Organizations.*

Peter's research, found in unpublished writings in my father's files, had concluded that educational institutions are desperately crying out for "moral based leadership that is not presented in sermon form," which was exactly what my father had been providing. Peter referred to what Norm had been doing as "the spiritual dimension of leadership." In his humble response, my father was heard saying, "I'm afraid he was a bit biased."

Peter summarized Norm's leadership style, then interviewed him extensively for his thesis.

> *Peter Dunkel:* These are observations on the unique personal qualities I found in Norm that make his leadership so powerful and effective:
>
> 1. Know your faith and values.
> 2. Cultivate a true sense of humility.
> 3. Respect your spouse and strive for an equal partnership.
> 4. Become an expert in your profession.
>
> Certain qualities consistently show through: honesty, transparency, humility, wisdom. Norm is a person with deep faith who does not wear it on his sleeve. His humility is genuine, so much so that I finally had to ask him how he is so successful. His response was pure Norm: "Oh, I was just an average college president, but I have a hell of a wife. We functioned as a team, and she was the one who made it a success."

Peter dug deeper into my father's leadership philosophies by asking him probing questions. The answers that follow reveal a wealth of insight and advice for anyone on the leadership path.

> *Peter:* What makes some leaders great?
>
> *Norm:* Leadership is all about character and values and consistency. Certain principles work anywhere, like vision, sacrifice, humility, servanthood. The best leaders have values which show up every day in their lives and work. For me, these are honesty, integrity, trustworthiness, and love.
>
> A leader must know their weaknesses and strengths, and not imitate somebody and expect to be successful. A vigorous self-examination is essential. Know yourself. Know how you think. Know yourself as others know you, and as we know them.

All leaders must have a vision and anticipate the future. The vision must be shared, and you must know how to build consensus with a team around that vision. If followers don't follow you, then you are not a leader. You need to teach them where you want them to go. It's an art form that is difficult to describe.

You've got to have an ego, or they will plow you under. Humility and confidence in forgiveness are marks of a true leader. Pride and ignorance of self can be your downfall.

I believe everyone can be a leader. We are all at various stages in experience and skills, and that is okay. Begin where you are.

Peter: How do leaders make decisions?

Norm: There were three ways I approach making decisions. First, I use my intuition; oftentimes you know when something needs immediate attention. Second, I postpone a decision as long as I can. Some things work themselves out, so intuitively you know when you can wait.

My institutional decision-making beliefs are not theory-based; instead, they cut through to the pragmatic. The three questions from the audit process I developed at American Lutheran Church shaped my decision-making at work: What needs to be done? What is currently preventing you from doing it? and Where do you start?

You can't bully your way through an organization, or you will get cut to ribbons.

Peter: How do people become leaders?

Norm: I was chosen to be president, I did not choose. This is the best way. Looking back on my life, I've found my actions were led by the spirit in a quiet, consistent sort of a way. I walked through open doors, and my faith gave me confidence.

Peter: Can leadership be learned?

Norm: Yes, and I'm the example that you can learn it. I was an introvert most of my life and did not find my calling until much later. I learned leadership by watching others during my years at ALC, observing more about what leaders should *not* do vs. what they should do. I learned how to get to the bottom line, to the truth, where real leadership needs to begin and to take charge.

Peter: How do you inspire people to change?

Norm: There are two ways to do this—through vision and through the "tremble factor." Roman arches used to fall and kill workers until they put the chief builder and architect under the arch when the scaffolding was removed; then the arches held and stopped falling. This level of accountability is the tremble factor: perform or get fired. If you don't change, you're out of a job.

Some people resist change, but give them a few years to come around. Plant the seeds for your vision. Some never change, so you learn to work around them. However, people generally don't like to feel they've been left behind, so they eventually fall in line.

A leader must see every person as a diamond in the rough. If you work with them to do their best, they can become that diamond. Unfortunately, if they don't, you must throw them out and get another person. They deserve a chance to discover what they are really good at, and that may require them to be somewhere else.

A leader should get to know people on their team on a personal basis—their families, goals, aspirations. They should give their people credit, tell others about all the great things going on, and then not take the credit.

If conflict arises, leaders meet with the person face to face to discuss it. No memos, no telephone calls, and no emails.

Leaders will find their days numbered if they become arrogant and bully people, believing they are the institution and not a person.

Peter: What are the bases of the leader's power and authority?

Norm: Power is not bad, but the way power is used is often inherently bad. For example, *sapiential authority*, the authority of wisdom and experience, rather than power based on position or status is the essence of leadership. It rests on competence and on confidence—your own, and that of others—that there is rightness, justice, wisdom, experience and other such attributes backing up decisions. The decisions are shared decisions, and the credit for work and progress is shared with all. Success comes with understanding that you are a more powerful leader when you share leadership.

There is another kind of power—simply by knowing you have power, and a good leader knows. Also, people know if you embody your values; if you do, then you have power.

Peter: What are the greatest joys of leadership?

Norm: Getting things done. Chalking up another goal and going for the next one. It was tremendously rewarding seeing people happy and proud of what they have accomplished. Bringing out the best in people, seeing their rise, was a source of great joy.

Peter: Do leaders feel accountable for what happens in their organizations?

Norm: Yes. Absolutely. When something went wrong, I took responsibility for it. The best way to deal with mistakes is to face up to them, tell the truth, and move on. Accountability as a leader is important all around.

For me, this is deeply rooted in my faith. We are sinners saved by grace, so I know that I am forgiven. I will continue to make mistakes my entire life, and I will continue to be forgiven. If you can't find some way to forgive yourself, you might as well forget it, because that's when the real problems start.

Peter: What are potential downfalls to effective leadership? How do you counteract them?

Norm: Despite all the drawbacks of ego, you must have a strong one. Your mindset must be, *I was selected for this job and I am going to do it.*

Great leaders have great egos tempered by realistic self-assessment, and they set aside personal goals. A good leader must see themselves as others see them and adjust to the needs of the people they are guiding toward what they perceive as their mission.

On the other hand, leaders can fall into the trap of not advancing their own ideas if they lead by too much consensus. This only works if all team members are bright and able. Since power abhors a vacuum, someone, or a small group, will work its will. Leaders need to bring a touch of order to chaos.

It is dangerous to let the ego get out of control. Little character flaws arise: not listening, not honoring others' ideas. Then, when change and adverse conditions arise, too strong an ego makes change more difficult. Frequent change can cause distress in spades if we do not change direction enough to let the currents of the time help us reach our goal.

A healthy ego has a sense of humor. The ability to laugh at oneself and one's foibles. In my case, it's my wife who keeps my feet on the ground.

Healthy self-confidence is generated by a concept of forgiveness and renewal every day. No need to look back or agonize. Move on.

> In summary, you may need a six-shooter for success in a Wild West movie, but you'll need to check it at the door when working with people in real life.

A balanced ego is like a dance. Norm modeled "leading from behind," as my brother Bill describes it. One must be incredibly confident to do this, and my father's faith and reliance on Spirit, his inner GPS, is what gave that confidence to him.

EGO CAN'T SLEEP. IT MICRO-MANAGES. IT DISEMPOWERS.
IT REDUCES OUR CAPABILITY. IT EXCELS IN CONTROL.
—ROBERT K. GREENLEAF

As interim president at Rockford College in Illinois, Norm started to step away from his humble "lead from behind" comfort zone, urging students to rise up and lead. It was 1992, and his voice rose as Iraq invaded Kuwait, and U.S. forces known as Operation Desert Storm struck back. Ethnic cleansing in Bosnia left everyone reeling. Closer to home, race riots broke out in Los Angeles after four white policemen were acquitted of beating to death an African American, Rodney King, in spite of videotaped evidence put on TV for all to see.

Only two weeks on campus at Rockford, Norm gave a "let her rip" speech to the graduating class, challenging students to be active leaders pushing for change. Jo wasn't there and hadn't heard the speech, but when she read it recently, she said to him, "I didn't realize, living with you all these years, that you were such a great man."

Here is an excerpt from that speech, given in 1992 to graduates at Rockford College:

> *Norm:* Today there is an accelerating pace and pervasiveness of change that is vaulting us breathlessly into a new

world orbit. You face emerging global economies, a breakdown of old theories and values before new ones can be put in place. You face a time when most leadership of our country and world is embedded in the patterns of the past, stuck in bureaucracy and holding back change.

Our opportunity is to see the good in change and work for the good. As you do, you dare not be absorbed into your self—your greed, your pride, your prejudice—not if you want to be a new age leader. You must learn to serve because it is in serving others that one best serves oneself.

Not that it is wrong to be successful, or to be rich and famous, nor to be single-minded in whatever goals you pursue. It is not wrong. But it is inadequate to take too much pride in achievement, too much ownership of material gain, and too little caring for the welfare of others.

Expect all kinds of trials and tribulations to assail you; welcome them as friends because they come to help you build character. It is most often the person who has been tried in the fires of adversity who builds character, who becomes wise and able to lead. The world ahead of you, the world ahead of all of us, needs leaders with character and moral backbone. Who among you will become a Moses, a Washington, a Lincoln, a Martin Luther King Jr?

Packing their bags again in 1993, Norm and Jo went off to Texas Lutheran College where he took to the podium calling for a new mission for our country, foretelling a future where we find ourselves in present day. Here is an excerpt from a speech he gave as the college's interim president:

Norm: I have been struggling with my sense of unease about where our society is heading. I mean our America. It is a problem for me when I vote for billionaire independent candidate Ross Perot as a protest against the lack of meaningful direction from establishment parties and candidates.

> We need to find a way to develop a new dream from the ashes, preferably before we are reduced to ashes. We need a genuinely new way of thinking about the mission of America, and how to reestablish some national and world goals.

GATHERING ON SANIBEL ISLAND

With nine grandchildren living in three states, my parents started a new tradition of bringing us all together for Thanksgiving week on Sanibel Island off the Gulf Coast in Florida. In the years between 1995 to 2005, each family rented a condo at Loggerhead Cay, and the many cousins had freedom to explore and bond through adventure.

Tennis, beachcombing, biking, and parasailing with Grandma (at the age of eighty!) were favorite activities, as well as sitting around the table after dinner playing card games, such as Up the River, Royal Rummy, or Hearts. Grandpa taught the kids to "smoke 'em," or when shuffling a deck to "cut them deep and sleep in the street, or cut them thin, and I will win." He was known to be gleeful when he won, and luck frequently followed him, much to everyone's frustration.

The grandchildren to this day quote "Grandpa-isms," Norm's famous adages. Granddaughter Leslie Horn Clark still uses "The dryer gets what the washer misses" when she and her husband Brad need a little extra elbow grease to complete a job. Andrew Fintel remembers Grandpa saying "That's just dirty pool" when he passed a speed trap on a freeway, calling out dishonesty as unsportsmanlike conduct when someone didn't play by the rules. Other favorites include:

"It's easier to ask forgiveness than permission."
"Often wrong, never in doubt."
"When fixing blame, first look in the mirror."
"When arguing with a fool, make sure you aren't similarly occupied."
"The first liar doesn't have a chance."
"Consider the source."

Happily entrenched with family and friends at the lake, mountains, or sea during these years, Norm and Jo could never have predicted where they'd go next. But as it turned out, they still had work to do in the world, and it was soon time for another courageous step through yet another unexpected open door.

QUESTIONS FOR SELF-REFLECTION

- Norm and Jo's family were everything to them. They made sure deep bonds were made. How do you do this in your own family?
- Grandparent influence can be transformational for children. Are you able to pass your values and family heritage down to your grandchildren? How do you do this? If they live some distance away, do you connect with Facetime or social media?
- Do you consider yourself a leader? Would you like to be a more effective leader?
- What characteristics do you see in people you think of as strong leaders?
- What are the qualities you see in people in leadership positions that weaken their effectiveness? And how do you interact with them? Is there anything you could be doing differently?
- Aphorisms were good as a teaching tool for Norm, an effective supplement to his parenting style of modeling behavior. Do you have any favorite adages reflecting your life views?

CHAPTER 14

Bountiful Harvest

A GREATER MISSION
(1997–2015)

THE WORLD IS ROUND SO THAT FRIENDSHIP MAY ENCIRCLE IT.
—PIERRE TEILHARD DE CHARDIN

AS GOOGLE BECAME A VERB and technology entered our lives, my father called the information revolution "one of the most convulsive changes of all times." The Internet placed real-time information at our fingertips, and with smartphones, face-to-face talking lost out to social media chatting—Facebook, Twitter, and Instagram, to name a few. My father would tell granddaughter and namesake Nora that real "face-time" meant a peck on the cheek and wasn't just an app on her smartphone.

Our country was brought to its knees as we watched hijacked planes fly into and bring down our World Trade Center in 2001. Turbulence hit our pocket books as the Dow Jones surged above 3,500 for the first time, then slid down as we lived through the biggest market crash in 2008 since the Great Depression, sending aftershocks around the world.

America elected our first African-American president, Barack Obama, who had the audacity to inspire hope, followed by the rise of the Tea Party, a populist movement. Voters were becoming increasingly polarized over issues such as health care, gun control, climate change, same-sex marriage, and legalizing pot.

The late '90s were nomadic years for my parents. They wouldn't settle down until at age eighty, health issues became the deciding factor. But first, their lives were interrupted when a chance meeting resulted in a rerouting of direction.

TANZANIA, AFRICA

Yet another unexpected call came when a door opened on an opportunity that would take them almost 8,000 miles away, this time to Moshi, Tanzania. Ten years after retiring and now seventy-three, my parents packed their bags and without a blink, hopped on a twelve-hour flight to a far-flung destination, again going to the heart of where they felt change was really happening, at the base of Africa's largest mountain, Mt. Kilimanjaro.

As Jo recalled about their decision, "We went to Africa on blind faith. We came home knowing that lives had been changed, including ours." Norm tells of how the spirit led him and Jo at the time:

> *Norm:* Looking back on my life, I find it hard to comprehend all the places we have been and all the experiences we have had. It wasn't until Jo and I were at Uhuru Hostel in Moshi, Tanzania, one day in 1998, looking out at Mt. Kilimanjaro, that I said to her, "How did we get here? I feel as if I've spent my whole life in preparation for this place. Here I can really use most of what I have learned."

Somehow the spirit had plowed through the accumulation of seasons past and was nurturing a seed, a small seed like the Biblical mustard, which would grow in time to become a tall and productive plant. With that revelation, I set out to do what I knew how to do, and trusted that if the principles and values I had lived by were honestly put forth, the spirit would grant an increase to my efforts. And that's exactly what happened.

In 1998, Jo met Pastor Anna, a visiting pastor from Tanzania, at choir practice at College Lutheran Church in Salem and told her we were interested in doing work overseas. That was at 9:30 pm. By the next morning, we had an email from Bishop Kweka of the Lutheran Northern Diocese of Tanzania, asking us to come. We packed our bags and set off for the unknown. It would be the first of three trips we would make to Africa.

The land of Tanzania is one of God's gifts to people, from the beauty of Mt. Kilimanjaro to the wild-like preserves of Ngorongora Crater to the Serengeti Plains. It is home to the Olduvai Gorge where discovered human remains are said to be 1.6 million years old, and modern research points to the possibility that Africa is indeed the birthplace of humankind. The Tanzanian people are proud of their peaceful history. Despite having 120 tribes, they do not war against each other as do tribes in neighboring African countries.

There had been an explosion of growth in the Lutheran churches in Tanzania, taking off from 2.5 million members to over 6 million in a short amount of time. At the same time, Lutheran churches in the U.S. had dropped half of our members. The Tanzanians had taken some giant steps of leadership, though they were understandably having trouble building schools and hospitals fast enough to keep up with demand.

Led by Bishop Kweka, the Northern Diocese had over 300,000 members, fifty-five schools, three hospitals, a women's center, and a home for disabled children. A laborer in that country might earn a dollar a day. Nearly everyone grows their own food. Like us in the Great Depression, they don't have money, but they are eating.

Tanzanians are tough-minded, intelligent, and happy people. They are determined to be leaders, finding how to serve their people in ways that are natural and true to the values and culture of Tanzania and Africa.

We soon learned that it was the women of the Masai tribe who were leading the change. For too long, women had existed as a nonentity in society, serving men while men were the big shots, seeing themselves as soldiers and warriors. The women grasped what needed to be done, then started programs that went after the excesses of the tribes and their vigilante approach of male dominance. They began changing the culture of the home and communities.

Knowing that not all wisdom resides in the West or the East, I see my task as that of a sower sowing seed, perhaps doing some weeding, helping nourish a new culture of planning. It is not up to me to worry about the harvest.

Remarkably, we found joy amidst the poverty and need that was all around us. There is a depth of spirit among these African Lutherans that I covet for myself, and it is obvious when in Tanzania, that happiness is not limited to the possession of wealth and material.

Our first visit was to get acquainted. Every morning a driver took us to a different place. We never knew where we were going. We visited a fish pond where people developed protein-based food sources. We went to the Kidia School on the slopes of Mt. Kilimanjaro where lessons were written on cheap blackboards and chalk was locked up after class—too expensive to be used foolishly.

At the end of our initial visit, Bishop Kweka asked us to return for four months to help them develop programs and training for their people to solve their own problems. I returned and did this in seminars and workshops, offering what I knew of personal and organizational effectiveness.

Bishop Kweka's team were in the Dark Ages about management but had an innate understanding of how to help people by helping them help themselves. Most of my work was planting seeds for future leadership, getting people to think about the future, not just the needs of the day.

At the end of four months, with so much more to do, I wrote a short book, *VIMIPUGOA*, to be used as a continuing resource for their work. My goal was to stimulate a way of thinking about planning and management with a simple message of hope and that change is possible.

Our time in Tanzania was life-changing in many ways. I knew that our American church and country were in trouble, especially after being in Tanzania and seeing there the difference in approach to caring for the welfare of the people. The zeal of the teachers, students, and parents was inspiring.

It is almost too easy to succeed in America. We are caught up with material goods and money, which does not add up to more happiness or satisfaction. We lack a consensus around a national vision and culture of success. We must find a common approach and strategy for influencing our national goals, beginning with education and health care.

With deep meditation and fervent prayer, we dare to dream boldly for the future of Tanzania, our nation, and the world.

MY OWN DOOR OPENS

While Norm and Jo were in Tanzania, my husband and I took our girls out of elementary school to visit them. It was a life-altering trip for all of us. Seeing how far the value of an American dollar stretched and experiencing the positivity of Tanzanians, changed our lives. Being invited to a public school and into the homes of hostel workers left lasting impressions. Greg and I donated $500 to one of the schools managed by the Lutheran synod, and within one year their graduates had the highest single score on the exams of any school in Tanzania.

I remember flying home from Tanzania with a new definition for "success." The kind of success I experienced in the Tanzanian culture did not equate to financial gain, although funding was needed for the people to achieve their dreams. I saw happiness, joy, and deep faith, and I wanted more of what they had.

Not long after returning from Africa, our family left Wisconsin and moved to Greenville, SC, and my earlier exposure to life in the Southeast helped me guide my daughters through a similar transition. Before buying a home, I visited nine schools, being undecided until a guidance counselor at J. L. Mann High School said something that caught in my heart. "We are a real-life experience," she told me. "Diverse in socio-economic status, intellectual abilities, and every color of skin." Perfect.

One of my first friends, Marsha Wallace, lived five doors down from the house we bought. Her friendship and partnership would later have a huge impact on the course of my life. Eventually we would co-found a nonprofit organization, Dining for Women, where I would be able to reach back across the ocean to Africa and help the women and girls I'd met in Tanzania. But first, an abrupt event would change forever the world as we knew it.

SEPTEMBER 11, 2001

Most of us vividly remember where we were on the morning of Tuesday, September 11, 2001, when the Islamic terrorist group

Al-Qaeda hijacked four planes and carried out their suicide attacks. Two of these planes flew into the Twin Towers in lower Manhattan, bringing down the World Trade Center.

Watching with increasing alarm the horror and violence spreading throughout the world, Norm reached out in a letter to his nine grandchildren with a message of hope, urging them to become leaders. His words speak to everyone.

> *Norm:* The week before September 11, I found myself humming a newer hymn, one entitled "Bind Us Together, Lord." Perhaps I sensed in some extraordinary way that the whole world was about to change, and it was preparing me for the tragedy to come. Perhaps it was coincidence. But then came September 11, and the tune came back with real vigor now added to its lyrics:
>
> *Bind us together, Lord,*
> *Bind us together with cords that cannot be broken.*
> *Bind us together, Lord, bind us together, Lord;*
> *Bind us together in love.*
>
> In the blindness of our outrage and sorrow, this tune gave me extra comfort because its words promise that love, not hate, makes the world go around. Love is a much harder act than the easier instruments of revenge and hate, but love, even as justice is pursued, is the only final answer.
>
> The world is indeed in travail. The battle between good and evil is joined with our substitution of personal and material welfare over the welfare of everyone. We must vow to do things differently. *We simply cannot stand idly by.*
>
> What else can we do?
>
> Now is the time for our young people to get involved in the processes of government. Now is the time for Julie, Leslie, Robert, Andrew, Stephen, Michael, David, Nora, and Jeanette to come to the aid of our world. It is safe

to dream, even if the dream is remote. I once dreamed of being president of the United States, and it didn't hurt me one bit to step aside to what I could do—at least I thought I could be president!

If you do not dream now—then when? If you do not dream now, who will?

If you do dream now, what will you do to make your dream happen—at school, in your life, in the world around you?

We trust that you will be able to live in a world as good as the one we have known. That can happen best if we "bind ourselves and our world together in love."

OUR CULTURE IS AT A CRITICAL CUSP—A TIME THAT REQUIRES WE DEFINE WHAT IT MEANS TO BE A CITIZEN IN A DEMOCRACY. WITHIN OUR NATION, WE NEED TO FOSTER A GREATER SENSE OF COLLECTIVE RESPONSIBILITY.
—ROBERT N. BELLAH, *HABITS OF THE HEART*

FAMILY AND LEADERSHIP: SOWING SEEDS OF ABUNDANCE

The next year, family and friends gathered at our Sand Lake cabin to celebrate Norm and Jo's fiftieth wedding anniversary. The weather cooperated, and we transformed the garage with white twinkling lights while a neighbor roasted a pig on a spit in his backyard. The grandkids decorated a float for the 4th of July Parade, featuring gold thrones and crowns for Grandma and Grandpa. As they rode their float through the streets, the children tossed candy and Mardi Gras beads to the eager crowds on the curbs in this one-traffic light community of Moose Lake.

Norm was seventy-seven when he answered the call again. This time the phone rang, and a headhunter asked if he'd step in as interim president at Lenoir Ryne University in Hickory, NC. "Do you know how old I am?" my father replied, a bit stunned that at his age, he was still needed to serve. But he accepted the job. To get my mother excited about going, he promised her a new car of her choice. This was a huge deal because he was so very frugal. She picked out a Prius, and off they went. This would be his last call answered.

At this time, my family and I were settled nearby in Greenville, South Carolina, both girls in school, in the 3th and 5th grade. I missed working and not having a sense of purpose outside of the home. I continued to struggle in my ordeal of living with increasing chronic pain, when a door opened for me, pointing the way to manage my pain through the distraction of doing good, a kind of mind control, in a sense. Doing good turned into a healthy addiction.

A DOOR OPENS IN MY LIFE

Ever since I returned home from Africa, I struggled with the discordance between needs and wants in my lifestyle in comparison to those of the people I'd met in Tanzania. Even more disquieting was witnessing the joy in their hearts and the depth of their faith in comparison to mine. So, when my neighbor, Marsha Wallace, invited me to celebrate her birthday in an unusual way, I discovered a way to reach back across the ocean and sustain mutually beneficial relationships. And like the doors that opened in my father's lifetime, this one was meant for me.

That night in January 2003, instead of *dining out* for Marsha's birthday, we *dined in* and donated the money we saved to Women for Women International, an organization profiled on Oprah. We decided to meet the next month, and this inaugural chapter of Dining for Women has been meeting every month ever since. Our simple model of raising awareness and collective giving resonated with people across the country and as we surged to 470 chapters, my father's steady hand was an unseen force guiding our organizational development.

Our chapter decided to support organizations focused on the well-being of women and girls living in the most impoverished countries in the world. I began researching how to get our donations into their hands. Looking back, I was searching for places where the need for change was palpable, where women and girls dwell in the most impoverished, marginalized corners of the world. Where opportunity never comes. I was following my father's example for making change at the heart of where change needs to begin. One of our first grants went to women and girls I'd met in Africa.

Norm once told me, "Look what's going on in Africa, what you're doing there. People are doing what works, working together, one woman at a time."

This was a time when I was going full speed ahead, and Norm began winding down. He turned his focus on adapting the book he'd written in Tanzania, *VIMIPUGOA*, for American audiences and publishing the book he'd started with Peter Dunkel on leadership.

EFFECTIVE LEADERSHIP: A GUIDE FOR CHURCH AND NONPROFIT ORGANIZATIONS

Effective Leadership: A Guide for Church and Nonprofit Organizations, published in 2004, was written for organizational leaders, though it was also loaded with transferable wisdom for individuals. Norm believed true leaders bring their values wherever they go—home, work, church, sports arenas, and even on the crowded freeways. The following highlights from his book provide a sample of his leadership philosophy:

> *Leadership skills cannot be picked up from supermarket shelves, and they aren't easily replicated. Leadership is ultimately personal and defies easy definition, even description. We all put our own spin on it. Your personal values define your style in a sense this is your plan for caring for other people. There is no conflict between your personal and professional values—they*

are the same. They must be if you are to have any integrity; otherwise, people will see right through you.

Practice to make your leadership skills fully operational. How often have you said to yourself after something went wrong, Now, I knew better than that! Put your values into the recesses of your mind, so they guide you in times of decision-making and stress. Practice makes perfect.

Remember that you are working with other humans in your home, community, and organizations. Each has a set of values most likely different from yours. Listen, find weaknesses, and find ways to arrive at the strongest commonly held values. Teamwork is a foundation stone for leadership.

All of us need something to get us started. We need tools, a list of instructions, even a starter kit. Use the Three Questions to start analyzing yourself and the things you want to get done: What's the problem? What's preventing you from solving it? and Where do we start? Extend those questions wherever you are—home, work, school—as a way of helping you focus on what really needs to be done.

Don't forget patience and the ability to learn from mistakes are two marks of a leader. Effective leaders are always searching for new, more, and better ways of getting the job done.

ROVING HOMES, 2004-2007

When my sister Peggy bought a second home in the mountains of Draper, a tiny town an hour south of Salem and ten minutes from my brother Bill's home on Claytor Lake, my parents sold their home and to the surprise of many, moved their belongings into Peggy's new home. They were still summering on Sand Lake and wintering at a condo Greg and I had bought in Perdido Key, FL. At Draper, they relished the spring and fall in a welcoming home where my father felt a keen sense of serenity and belonging, amid a private sanctuary with the beauty of God's earth on full display.

In 2007, when a few health scares caught up with them at Sand Lake, my parents sold their cabin—a heart-wrenching decision—and moved ten minutes away from where I lived in Greenville, SC. The move placed them solidly between Peggy in Atlanta and Bill in Virginia. It wasn't long after that Jo would need open heart surgery to replace her aortic valve.

During these years, Norm, a pacifist at heart, became dismayed by the rise of extremism, and his heart ached when a school shooting rampage hit close to home, leaving thirty-three students dead on the campus of Virginia Tech. Donald Trump's TV show "The Apprentice" hit the airwaves, and Norm shunned reality TV which he saw as mirroring a decline in American values.

So much was churning in the world: a bomb targeted runners at the Boston Marathon, and terrorists attacked the American embassy in Benghazi, Libya. Russia annexed the Ukrainian territory of Crimea, causing widespread condemnation, and in horror we witnessed the birth of ISIS.

Back home, infrastructure fault lines were exposed in Minnesota with the collapse of the I35 bridge over the Mississippi River, and black Freddie Gray died while in custody of the police in Baltimore.

We also celebrated the fifty-year anniversary of Martin Luther King Jr's "I Had a Dream" speech, calling us back to his peaceful path to unity, and amazingly, a 3-D printer would grow a human ear.

It wasn't long before Norm started having troubling dreams about extremism and division in the world, an omen for things to come. This was the moment he decided to write a book of hope for his grandchildren, to share his lessons learned and family history, inspiring them to be leaders in their lives and to live to serve others. That book evolved into what you now hold in your hands, a collaborative labor of love that almost reached completion in his last year of life but would benefit from the greater perspective of seeing his life in retrospect.

He also found hope in the work of Dining for Women, as we hit periods of exponential growth. People were crying out for ways to put our country and world back on a path of unity, and our model was proving that collective donations and individual actions, when multiplied by thousands, was proving that the way our world works can be changed. What I've witnessed in building a movement of like-minded people is that our differences fall away as we find unity in our hearts—where we are all the same. One individual can change the world, and it all begins with ourselves. This is what I learned from Norm.

FAMILY EVOLUTION

To the delight of Jo and Norm, our family kept expanding. Leslie was the first grandchild to marry, choosing Brad as her life partner. Then Andrew married Amy, followed by Stephen marrying Jessica and Julie marrying Chris. Great grandchildren arrived, beginning with Silas; then came more bundles of joy—Emma, Viviana, and Lilah. A year later, we welcomed Luke and Will, and Stephen and Jessica are now expecting.

BRANDON OAKS, VIRGINIA

As they approached ninety, in 2014, my parents felt called "home" and moved to Brandon Oaks, a Lutheran retirement center close to Roanoke College in Virginia. They moved away from Peggy and me, and it was Bill and Connie's turn to benefit from having them close by.

Salem and the Roanoke Valley welcomed them back to the loving community which had first opened its doors nearly forty years earlier. Life was rich with interactions and deeply meaningful relationships. Norm was home.

When the family decided to surprise him for his ninetieth birthday, Roanoke College President Mike Maxey opened the doors of the President's Home for our celebration.

Ever the quiet introvert, Norm transformed into a talker and man of action. The college set up an office in the Fintel Library where he could work on his book. At Brandon Oaks, he grew tomatoes and spent hours weeding and pruning the flower beds. He played bridge, walked the halls, worked jigsaw puzzles, and listened to people tell their stories.

> *Norm:* Well, I put puzzles together with other people who are puzzlers, and I sit and talk to them, and try to help them understand who they are. They had some great stories to tell—it's not a normal distribution curve. This capstone age group had a lot of wisdom. I found out who people really are and tried to make them feel good about themselves, because if they do, then we all think better of others.
>
> Being in a retirement center with hundreds of similar lives and tales has shaped my thinking and made me grateful to be in their company. Everyone lives through at least one lifetime challenge, and I learned from them about how varying levels of faith—deep, insufficient, inconsequential—played a role in rising to the challenges. We just don't know how to grasp at some force so powerful and yet benign, one which cannot be explained by science as "accidental," because the odds are too great!

My father's disturbing dreams continued. Getting his book written took on a sense of urgency, as he witnessed declines in societal values and unprecedented levels of discord among our leaders. He was so disturbed that on September 24, 2015, he wrote Bishop Elizabeth Eaton, head of the Evangelical Lutheran Church of America. Here is an excerpt from that letter:

> *Norm:* After hearing Pope Francis speak to the U.S Congress, I have no doubt that the spirit is once again at work within the Catholic Church. I keep waiting to see him retreat or be overshadowed by the "Establishment" in Rome, yet instead of losing battles, he is winning in ways no one could have predicted. So I decided I needed to vent and take some positive action.

I am writing to plead for similar leadership in the Lutheran Church, so that we help solve and reverse the secularization trends of cultures around the world. I offer my assistance, if appropriate, but I also offer my support and prayers for your wisdom and insight for the future of our Church in America. But what can I do to help? I am too old to "dig in," and my wife is ninety and cannot travel. I am best at private, confidential conversations.

Our prayer is that you, like Solomon, will be given wisdom and understanding in your time of leadership.

But what can I do to help? Norm didn't realize it, but this question had set him on the path to share his life lessons in a book. This is that book, his message of hope. Why I had to finish it for him was because, for the first time, a door opened that my father didn't want to walk through. The first clue was a slight pain in his sternum that wouldn't go away.

QUESTIONS FOR SELF-REFLECTION

- Do you have an idea of what you will do when you are retired? Or if you are already retired, how do you spend your time? Is there a leadership component? An active way to reach out and touch the lives of others?
- Where were you on 9/11? How did your global view change? What is that view today? What are the ideas you think would help restore harmony and unity in our country and the world? Are you doing something to help? Are you seeking ways to help?
- Norm and Jo were anchors for the extended family. What is your role in your own family? How does your family deepen bonds? Who drives those relationships? What might you do differently to further them?

CHAPTER 15

Planting the Future

PASSING ON THE CALL FOR DOING GOOD (2016–2017)

THE TIME IS RIGHT TO DO WHAT IS RIGHT.

—MARTIN LUTHER KING JR.

IN 2016, A FINAL DOOR OPENED FOR NORM TO ENTER. I remember when he and Jo were staying with us for Christmas in 2015, and he went to bed unusually early, at 6:30. Earlier that year, he had lost ten pounds and endured months of nagging pain in his sternum, putting my physician brother Bill's radar on high alert.

After he was admitted to the hospital and had an MRI, my father received a visit from Bill's oncology partner, Dr. Paul Richards. He came into my father's hospital room and quietly closed the door before telling us that Norm had stage 4 non-smoker lung cancer. Later that day, when the hospital chaplain visited and asked my father about his preference for resuscitation, he said, "I need to live so I can take care of Jo."

I left the room to tell my mother and sister the news, and we began the rollercoaster of cancer, a lonely journey that is hard to understand unless you are along for the ride.

It was a time when the news media obsessed over politics, and negative stories were nearly all we heard. Unprecedented political acrimony and a rising freedom to espouse hate seemed to take our government and voters hostage. Some of the loudest leaders moved away from values-based leadership, a slippery slope for humanity. This "new normal" was so disturbing to Norm that he didn't want to leave this earth without assurance that hope existed in the next generations and that they were prepared to be leaders in the world around them.

This chapter is a reflection of how my father spent his final nine months, with examples that demonstrate that living Norm's Way is transformative for both the individual and the world around us. Equally as important in telling Norm's story are moments I can only describe as glimpses of the spirit at work in his life. In writing his story, my eyes were opened to see how much the spirit dwelt within him ever since he was just a small boy on the farm in Nebraska. They caught me by surprise because while my father was a deeply religious person, my own spiritual journey did not follow his. And yet, these remarkable, inexplicable moments have no easy rational explanation. They've changed my life, and I'll spend it seeking the same truth he sought, though I won't ever be able to replicate his goodness. At the least, I want to wake up every morning and try my best.

WE ARE NOT HUMAN BEINGS HAVING A SPIRITUAL EXPERIENCE, WE ARE SPIRITUAL BEINGS HAVING A HUMAN EXPERIENCE.

—PIERRE TEILHARD DE CHARDIN

MIRACLE NINE MONTHS OF LIFE

The first three months after Norm's diagnosis were a blur. Radiation, chemotherapy, and new breakthrough drugs had mixed a deadly cocktail. After one round of chemo, we nearly lost him. In three months, he'd lost thirty-six pounds and was prepared for the inevitable. As strange as it seems, his insurance paid for cutting-edge immunotherapy only after chemo failed.

Peggy and I took turns caretaking every other week, and the loving embrace of family and friends flowed in and out of my parent's apartment, proving love is the very best medicine.

By early April (Norm referred to it as April Fool's Day) in 2016, his appetite returned as the IV drips unleashed an army of T-cells that soon began winning the battle. Suddenly he was in remission. By July, we were all speechless when an MRI showed a hole had been blasted through the middle of the biggest tumor in his left lung. Who says there's no such thing as a miracle? His energy returned and so did his determination to finish writing the message he wanted to leave to the world.

We quickly got down to the business of finishing his book. It was the same month when Napster founder and Facebook mogul Sean Parker announced his $250 million donation for researching how our immune systems held the key to curing cancer. Norm was living proof that a sea change was coming in the world of cancer treatment.

HERE'S A CLUE TO FIND WHETHER YOUR MISSION ON EARTH IS FINISHED: IF YOU'RE ALIVE, IT ISN'T.

—RICHARD BACH (QUOTE FROM A CRYPTOQUOTE PUZZLE THAT NORM SOLVED DURING AN IMMUNOTHERAPY TREATMENT)

A MIRACLE MESSAGE

From listening and learning about Norm's lifetime, I understood he was a visionary, seeing beyond the moment, to what might be. *What might be* is the bright shining star that guided his life. A visionary sees what's possible and thrives by being resilient and knowing how to adapt in an ever-changing world. It's ironic that my father's name, *Norm*, is a word defined by Merriam-Webster as "a behavior standard for what is typical and acceptable." Norm was a natural born leader, who at the end of life, called for ethical and moral "norms" to prevail in how we lead our lives and in the leaders we elect to represent the people. He asks us to evaluate our lives, the values that define us, and carry those values with us wherever we go.

After a lifetime of encouraging others to "find our place to stand," in his final months we spoke about the values that defined his life. Keep in mind that his values are not necessarily transferable. We all get to choose the moral code by which we live. Here is a summary of Norm's top values, with definitions we culled from the Urban Dictionary:

- Honesty: Telling the truth consistently, a quality that most people seem to be missing these days. A moral, philosophical quality that you can't buy at Walmart.
- Integrity: Doing the right thing, even when nobody is looking. Doing what you said you would do.
- Trustworthiness: The ability to be relied on as honest or truthful. Dependable.
- Agape Love: A universal love to everybody without prejudice, without consideration of their worthiness to be loved. A universal love of humankind.
- Openness: Willing to listen to and hear an opposing or contradictory view. Even when you think you are right, you know that you can be wrong.

BE SURE TO PUT YOUR FEET IN THE RIGHT PLACE,
THEN STAND FIRM.
—ABRAHAM LINCOLN

WORDS FROM THOSE WHO LISTENED

During Norm's miracle year of remission, friends and loved ones reached out in love to him, each one a potent dose of medicine for his soul. Their stories exemplify the influenced Norm had in their lives, proving that living Norm's Way can be transformative.

> *Peggy Fintel Horn:* The biggest impact Dad had on my life was his completely trusting nature. He looked for the good in everyone and usually found it.

President of Roanoke College Mike Maxey asked alumni and friends to share stories of Norm's influence in their lives. Hundreds poured in, illustrating by their remarks how my father's legacy lives on. Here's a brief sampling of what people contributed:

> *Bill Nabers (Roanoke College alumnus) in his article "Confession" from the Mountain Courier, May 2017:* I miss his [Norm's] leadership in our currently emotionally driven, confrontational society that mistakes bluster and emotional expression for strength. His example is still a breath of fresh air blown by the spirit into my life.

> *Galdino "Dino" F. Pranzarone, faculty member:* In our passage through this mortal plane, we can be takers, watchers, or leavers. The takers deplete the world. The watchers are passive observers. The leavers are those who benefit both the world and their fellow men by their works and contributions to the welfare and happiness of those who know them, or those whom they served, directly or indirectly.

Courtney Kuel Johnson, Class of '92: I hope you know how much good you did and what an enormous difference you made to countless numbers of young minds. I'm betting most of us went forward to do great things and make a difference in someone else's life.

Tom Turner, Class of '83 and staff member: You had vision, set the bar high, and we truly stood on your shoulders in the years following graduation.

LIFE'S MOST PERSISTENT AND URGENT QUESTION IS WHAT ARE YOU DOING FOR OTHERS?
—MARTIN LUTHER KING JR.

A month before Norm died, he received a call from the African-American basketball players who he'd championed while they were students at Roanoke. This national title winning team, now came together, and each member got on the phone to express feelings of gratitude that were a powerful balm to Norm's spirit. Kenny Belton hosted the call and spoke for all when he told both my parents that the encouragement and hope they'd provided during their undergraduate years changed the trajectories of all their lives. This was the team that never lost a game, won the conference, and, as students, always had an open door to the president's office. Kenny and Gerald Holmes describe Norm's influence in the phone call.

Gerald Holmes: I was in trouble the second semester of my freshman year, and you vouched for me so I wouldn't need to go to summer school. Your belief and trust in a little kid out of DC taught me to survive a lot of obstacles in my life. I learned how to persevere which led to my success now. When I reflect back, this was monumental in my life.

Kenny Belton: The first time I visited campus, I didn't see enough black students. I said to Coach Green, "I'm looking for a college with more diversity, so I'll probably pass." He said, "Okay, but there's going to be some others here this term," so I enrolled.

That first year, there were six black guys and two black girls on campus. Before going home after our first semester, we all got together to check in and asked: Is everybody coming back? Everyone said yes.

The experience of having first-hand access to the president and Jo made the difference in our lives. Because of their support, we felt confidant recruiting other black students. I started working in the Admissions Office, and every time we'd talk with a student or player, we'd tell them, if there's any problem, you can go straight to the college president and talk with him. His door is always open.

Kenneth Belton graduated in 1981 and remains the top basketball shooter in Roanoke College history. He has received multiple awards for exemplary moral leadership and was recently elected to the college's board of trustees.

Two weeks after receiving the team's call, my parents were to attend a special ceremony where they'd be given the college's highest honor, the Roanoke College Medal. These beloved basketball players would all fly in to surprise my parents and attend the ceremony. Heartbreakingly, my father died five hours short of him being able to greet them, but there's no question that his legacy lives on in each one.

FINAL WEEKS

When cancer once again started winning the battle, Good Samaritan Hospice stepped in and helped Norm walk through his final door. Norm had two items on his bucket list: Living to April 7, when he and Jo would receive the prestigious Roanoke College

Medal and attending my daughter Jeanette's wedding on April 27.

In those last few weeks of life, we didn't turn on the tape recorder much. We just talked. But I did capture his words when remarking on his last wish for all, the parting words of a man who cared, led through Spirit, and inspired so many.

> *Norm:* Like a farmer in early spring, planting seeds for the dream of what can be when summer comes, we can build a forest of youth where the mind and world of humankind can grow to a new flowering, unknown and almost unthinkable to our present generations.
>
> While there is always another season for those of us here on earth, for those departing, it's an eternity of new seasons. My time is passing, and I leave you with thanks and love to all who cared, and my belief that hope will lead us to joy. God bless you. My peace I leave with you all.

SPIRITUAL EXPERIENCES

I've heard that when someone is near death, the layer between heaven and earth becomes thin and porous. That makes sense of the many inexplicable experiences I had, what I call "spirit sightings," before and after his passing. The timing and sheer number of these events radically changed my beliefs.

In my father's final days, a few incidents stand out as having this kind of spiritual significance. In one, as I sat by his side in their Brandon Oaks apartment and we talked about his life, I asked him what it felt like to live with an internal light of joy all his life. That revelation was so deeply personal for this humble, private man, that he rushed from the room, leaving me wondering if I'd intruded too far into his mind and heart.

Ten minutes later, he rushed back into the room, leafing through his old, red Lutheran hymnal to find the hymn, "Just As I Am." He told me this was the hymn he wanted sung at his funeral. I took note, but what happened next I can only explain as the spirit directing me.

Early in the evening, Peggy arrived to take over caretaking, relieving me to head out and drive home. I was packed and ready to go when something wouldn't let me leave. I decided to stay and rented the guest room for an overnight, but when I unlocked the door and walked in, I just couldn't stay separated from my family. After returning the key to the front desk, intending to return to my parents' apartment, I walked by the community chapel where a service was underway.

At first, I thought I was imagining it, but I wasn't. Inside the chapel, packed with so many of the friends my parents had made, people were singing the hymn "Just As I Am."

I was pulled into the chapel through the open door, and finding a seat in the back, I sat there with tears streaming down my face. When the service was over, I tried to hurriedly sneak away, but a long-time friend of my parents grabbed hold of me and assured me that faith and hope would see me through the loss of my father. She was right.

Another example of such spirit sightings is this: Late one evening, in my last unrecorded conversation with my father, I had placed my iPhone out of reach on a table across the living room. We were grappling with the meaning of life and how to equip the next generation of leaders for the world today, which is the ultimate message of this book. While we were having this conversation, Siri spoke from across the room, announcing via my iPhone: *Looking up the definition in Wikipedia for "Spirit of God."* We held each other's eyes in wonder, needing no words, understanding a greater force of goodness was at work in the world. In that moment, I believe, he knew he had done all he could in his time on earth and that his legacy was safely ensconced in the hands of the generations to come. With that realization, Norm felt the peace he needed in order to let go and be with God. As for me, I was left speechless and wanting more.

FINAL DAY

On April 6, one day before the medal ceremony, Norm was admitted to the hospital in the wee hours of the morning. My brother Bill happened to be the on-call physician. Family members arrived later that day and the next morning, expecting to attend the medal ceremony at noon on April 7. Instead, through the night, we took turns sitting at Norm's bedside.

My father passed away in the early morning on April 7, five hours before realizing his goal of living to receive the Roanoke College Medal. His nurse, who volunteered to be with him on her day off, told us she heard him say these words: "Not many people can look back on their lives and say, *I wouldn't change a single thing.* How lucky am I. I got everything I needed to get done in my final miracle year."

Ever since the morning he found me reading the Book of Daniel, I understood my father was ready to be with God. In a true example of his love and kindness for other people, he expressed feeling guilty that he would experience the joy of Eternal Life and those of us left behind would not. Typical, unselfish Norm, always worried about others before himself.

With the whole family gathered, my mother, a pillar of strength, asked us all to go to the ceremonial luncheon where she would accept the award for them both. This event was four hours after my father died. Walking in, we saw the Four Horsemen basketball players who flew in to surprise my parents. Jo asked Kenny Belton to join the family table, sitting in my father's place, a moving gesture that didn't go unnoticed. There was not a dry eye as she spoke to the audience, reminding us that love, courage, and leadership are a choice, the decision to take them up resting with each of us.

A CELEBRATION OF LIFE

It made sense to hold the funeral the next day after the award ceremony, with the family all gathered, though I can't imagine how Sally Walker, director of special events, and the college managed get the chapel and reception ready for hundreds of people during a busy Alumni Weekend.

We'd told my father we weren't going to wear black to his funeral, and the word spread. We entered a chapel that was alive with color. Tears were shed of sorrow and in celebration of one man's life lived well.

The eulogies were remarkable. College President Mike Maxey spoke of my father's unshakeable and unimpeachable integrity as a servant leader who quietly went about unlocking people's potential, and how he breathed energy and force into a vision for the future. My brother Bill's words were memorable: "Dad was always, *always* kind and thoughtful. 'Do the right thing,' he told us, 'and reflect that in your life.'"

My sister Peggy, as the oldest sibling, spoke to the grandchildren, passing Norm's baton to the next generation to serve as compassionate leaders in an ever-changing world. He would have loved seeing little Emma, his great granddaughter, escape from her mother and run up to Peggy as she spoke, demonstrating the energy of youth. Peggy spoke of our father as her hero, mentor, and quiet guide in her life. She acknowledged that growing up, we three children had shared him with thousands of others and somehow were never jealous because it meant we had more family. Peggy called on us to live out Norm's legacy, changing the world one person at a time, to take on being that force of change in our own lives.

Pastor Paul Hendrickson spoke next, taking us back to Nebraska to the farm, the heritage, where the spirit found my father, and my father found God. He reminded us that Norm was a Midwestern farmer at heart with an uncommon vision to see in others what they could not see in themselves, always looking past the ordinary to view the extraordinary, to what others had not yet imagined.

On the night of his funeral, Roanoke College celebrated its 175th anniversary with festivities that included fireworks lighting up the sky. We all felt that Norm was sent off in fitting style with such a generous celebration and love.

For my father, Eternal Life is his bountiful harvest. May we all live our lives with no regrets. His ashes are interred at the Roanoke College campus, in a garden setting at the base of the steps leading to the Fintel Library. My mom would join him when it was time. Inscribed on a bench overlooking the garden are the words my parents leave for the students and anyone who might want to change their life story: *We believe in you.*

AFTER DEATH SPIRIT SIGHTINGS

Jo moved in with me one week after Norm's funeral. She became my support for completing his book, although my father communicated with me as well—or his Spirit did. Whatever you call these experiences, I've learned from them that I don't know nearly as much as I thought I did. A higher power is at work.

Here are a few more spirit sightings that happened to me and to others in the days after Norm passed.

BEAMS OF SUNLIGHT IN A THUNDERSTORM

The morning my father died, I was driving through a storm to pick up a prescription for Jo. The mountains weren't visible through the heavy thunderclouds, and yet I witnessed a beam of sunlight coming through them, lasting several seconds. It startled me, and the thought occurred that it was a message from Norm, telling me all is well in Eternal Life. As I shook off that thought as unlikely, another sunbeam broke through the clouds, as if to pierce my doubting mind, and I knew it was true. He was smiling down on all of us.

BIRD PRESENCE

An avid bird watcher, Norm, it seemed, was communicating with us through this species. After the funeral service, Sally Walker, the college staff person who'd pulled together all of the funeral arrangements, described hearing a chorus of birds bursting into song while she stood in the back of the chapel. She wondered if we heard them, too. Norm loved birds.

Two weeks after the funeral, my younger daughter Jeanette married Gabriel in an outdoor garden setting in Greenville, SC. This was the second event on my father's bucket list. At the rehearsal, a pesky cardinal was swooping around our heads, expressing what seemed like annoyance at our presence. We discovered its nest in a tree next to the bar. Then, at the end of the rehearsal dinner, a waitress asked me if I'd seen the cardinal that followed me up to the front door, attempting to come in when I entered but not making it. That same bird then flew to the back door where the waitress was entering and tried to get in again. That night, Gabriel was "pestered" by a cardinal in the parking lot of his hotel while he was bringing in his luggage. The bird was so determined to get his attention that Gabriel took a photo of it.

Joyful and persistent birds, sunbeams piercing the darkened clouds: how could this be anything other than the spirit confirming Norm's continued presence in our lives? He found ways to reassure us that he was where he thought he would be, content in the "seasons of eternity."

There were more of these spirit sightings, many as I grappled with completing "our" book in the days after his passing.

REBIRTH OF A GERANIUM

There were times I felt overwhelmed and doubted my ability to finish the book. Discovering and reading through the 470 documents my father had gathered exhausted me. Some of the book's chapters were referenced by over sixty writings that could be included, requiring me to make some hard decisions. In those moments of doubt, signs appeared, giving me courage and confidence to keep on telling his story.

One such sign was the revival of my dead geranium plant, my father's favorite bloom. Unlike my father, I'm not known for my gardening talents, and most of my plants die early from insufficient nourishment. After he died, I bought a geranium plant for my deck which sadly shriveled and turned brown from neglect. Jo removed all the dead blooms, and the next day, when I was on the verge of giving up on writing, six red blossoms got my attention. A dead plant coming back to life overnight could only be explained in a spiritual dimension. I got back to finishing the task.

A month later, I hit another slump and didn't get out of my pajamas for several days. That's when I saw a hummingbird drinking nectar from all six blooms of the geranium. When the hummingbird finished, it hovered at eye level with me through the glass door, until I realized this was another message from my father, telling me to get over myself and finish the book. *Pick yourself up, Barb. Don't just stand there, write!* Instantly, the hummingbird vanished.

THE POWER OF THE INDIVIDUAL

As he wished it to be, Norm's legacy is that it's up to each of us to choose a life of purpose and action. His life lives on through us doing this.

My brother Bill sums it up well, saying, "He taught me to never consider myself the most important person in the room, even if I'm alone. There is something fascinating about every person you meet, and sometimes you have to dig for it. Don't lie to yourself. "*What good is a half-baked potato?*"

Bill's son Andrew, following in his own father's footsteps as an oncologist and who was with Norm in his final days, aspires to the same depth of faith Norm had. He aims to live up to that expectation not only for himself, but also for his own children and their future. Andrew adds that he misses Grandpa's waffles, the billions of pancakes, and especially the potato dumplings—adding his only regret is that he should've gotten the recipe.

For me, if I never do another thing, I pray for the habit of seeing the good in people, not passing judgment on what is different and being curious enough to find out. I'm humbled and grateful to say that Norm's legacy lives on in the work I do through Dining for Women, empowering individuals to take action and be part of a movement opening doors of opportunity for women and girls globally.

I know I'm only one person in thousands he inspired, and that his legacy lives on in each of us who take up the mantle of service to others. My hope is that like him, you dedicate yourself to walking, not only talking, your values, taking them with you on your journey through life, wherever you may go, and changing the world—one person at a time.

LET'S ALL LIVE WITH NO REGRETS.
—BARB FINTEL COLLINS

QUESTIONS FOR SELF-REFLECTION

- What do you think is going on in the world today? Listen to the interpretation of your children and grandchildren. Talk to people who don't share your views. If you do, might your views change?
- As one individual, have you found ways to help bring about unity to our country and the world in this divisive time? Is there a discourse in your own family, and with friends and work colleagues about it? If not, where might you begin?
- Are the right leaders in place in your community, state, and national government? Do you agree with a need for more servant leaders? What qualities do you feel are most important in our leaders today?
- Our youth are growing up experiencing a sea change in how we communicate and hear the news. The younger generation is arising, becoming active in demanding social change. What might older generations learn from them? And how might older generations help shape these young leaders?

CHAPTER 16

Living Norm's Way

LOSING JO AND LIVING HIS LEGACY

DON'T JUST STAND THERE. DO S

—NORM FINTEL

ONE WEEK AFTER NORM DIED, J
HER NEW ROOM IN MY HC
CAROLINA. I promised my father I
of her, and for sixteen months sl
life, laughter, and her opinions or
my daily routine. Most days she'd
"Is it done yet?" In a way only a mother can, her pressure to finish it is a large part of why it got done. I think she was meant to outlive Norm so that she could take on the production phase of my writing and spice up his stories. I believe that this book extended each of their lives, neither letting

lovenorm.com

My DFW story begins on pgs 220, 223 & Ch 16

go until they were certain they'd had their say, and that Norm's message would be revealed to the world.

As Jo's heart lost its ability to sustain life, hospice once again entered our doors. In her last week of life, the final manuscript of the book was completed. In her last three days of life, I read it aloud while she squeezed my hand in the parts she loved the most. Cradled in love, holding our hands, Jo passed ten minutes after I finished reading the last word on the final page. I can only imagine she was anxious to go tell Norm all about it. My eternal hope is that, as only a mother can, she approved of how it turned out.

When Norm first asked me to write this book, my initial reaction was to say okay, though I remember feeling like a deer caught in the headlights, thinking I'm in way over my head, and that it may never get done. Then I discovered 470 of his lifetime writings, never seen before, and realized what he had to say just might be the answer to what we are all craving to know: how to restore harmony and optimism in the world we live in today. I realized that Norm was far from *norm*al, and his message was a gift to the world that needed to be told. Savoring each word of his wisdom, I tapped into my fearless gene to weave together his life story and message—a rallying cry for unleashing goodness in the world.

In the writing process my own life was transformed. First, about midway through, I realized I've been walking in my father's footsteps without knowing it. And second, I realized I had a long way to go before I could keep up with him. Having taken detours and traveled down many dead end roads in my life, I always had a beacon named Norm calling me home. I knew I needed to examine and make changes in my own life if I had any chance of living with the joy that encapsulated his life. So I asked myself his three questions, and in ruminating on the answers, I found a better way to lead my life. If I can do this, flawed as I am, there is hope for anyone to do it, as well.

I know how lucky I was in the parent lottery. Perhaps the most inspiring value I observed in Norm was his ability to see the best in everyone, and how he quietly and expertly maneuvered us to discover it for ourselves. And in Jo, it was her ability to look inside someone and see what may need healing, and giving everyone a safe and loving place to be their true selves. My parents' bold decision to move into the inner city and expose Peggy, Bill, and me as young children to real life in all its many colors and ways, taught me that what lies within is more important than what is visible on the outside. They taught me that changing the world is a dream worth chasing and shaped me to be a fearless advocate for compassionate social change.

A LEGACY OF EQUALIZING DOORS OF OPPORTUNITY

Equality of humankind is one of the greatest issues of our century. It was the overriding mission for my father's life. It became mine as well.

While Norm's path led him into higher education, mine led me to the nonprofit sector, where rewards correlate to the number of lives changed rather than the mighty dollar. It's where I found my calling for visioning what might be and for finding ways to make it happen. Lessons I learned from my father.

In 2003, when my neighbor invited me to celebrate her birthday by dining in with friends and pooling our dining out dollars to donate to women in need, I discovered a way to mobilize a people movement capable of co-creating a more just and peaceful world. This original group of women, the first Dining for Women chapter, has gone on to meet every month, learning about and funding women-led solutions to those stubborn doors of inequality scattered throughout the world. One of our next donations invested in the lives of the women I'd met in Tanzania, who displayed a steely determination for making a better life for their children and communities.

In 2005, a *New Ventures in Philanthropy* research study on giving circles fueled exponential growth in our model of engaged philanthropy. For several years, Dining for Women was spotlighted through extensive, unsolicited media coverage, and it didn't take long to build our movement from one to 470 chapters around the country. Fifteen years later, more than 32,000 people have invested over $7 million to projects in 60 countries that take down barriers restricting a person's ability to improve their lives simply because of where they were born, or that they were born a woman.

Through our emphasis on education, our eyes are opened to understanding why the majority of the world's poor and illiterate are women. Through our emphasis on collaboration and leadership development, our model harnesses the collective wisdom of our members as we transform into potent agents of change and global citizens. By aligning our efforts with the United Nation's Sustainable Development Goal number five—gender equality—we partner with allies working to remove gender-based barriers to economic empowerment and well-being by investing in critical programs in several areas, including education, healthcare, safety and security, leadership programs, and sustainable agriculture. We nurture a global conversation on why an investment in a woman's or girl's future, living in the most marginalized corners of the world, is a catalyst for the well-being of all people.

As a co-founder of this people movement, I often wonder, *Who am I, an ordinary person, to help lead this organization filled with extraordinary leaders and accomplished women and men?* Then I remember that the beauty of Dining for Women is that it doesn't matter if I am just an ordinary person, because Dining for Women is a great equalizer. It strips away our differences and unites people where it matters most—in our hearts. The place where we are all the same. We transform ordinary into extraordinary champions, mobilizing people to act as one. Our model gains momentum with each person who joins us. Because we have no minimum donation requirement and we shun labels, we offer equal opportunity for anyone to sit at the table where change is served up on a platter. When we do this, shifting the balance of equity in the world is possible.

THIS IS MY WAY OF EXTENDING THE LEGACY OF MY FATHER.
—BARB FINTEL COLLINS

A FUTURE ASSURED

Throughout the history of Dining for Women, my father's guiding hand was in the background at times of turbulence and triumph. He was with us at our 10th anniversary celebration, and would have been proud had he lived to attend our 15th Knowledge is Power Conference, held at the United States Institute of Peace (USIP) in Washington, DC. He would have loved hearing USIP president Nancy Lindborg, another Minnesota native whose father attended the same inner-city high school that I did, tell me that USIP has introduced peace and conflict studies into academic curriculum at all levels, from elementary to higher education. Imagine Norm's comfort knowing that USIP envisions a "world without violent conflict," and promotes human rights, justice, and the principles of democracy. I imagine he'd be ecstatic knowing that a high school textbook section on gender and peace-building led a young woman to start a DFW chapter in her high school.

Two stories illustrate the future of Dining for Women. They demonstrate the inspiring power of young people rising up as agents of change in their communities and throughout the world.

When Naserian was 14, as she walked home from church in rural Kenya, she was kidnapped, raped, and forced into an arranged marriage. Her uncle helped rescue her, but the next day when fetching water from the river, she was kidnapped again and forced to assume the role of a wife. This time, one of Naserian's teachers asked Kakenya's Dream, an organization supported by Dining for Women, to help, and when Naserian was found, they gave her a safe place to sleep, and get support and encouragement to continue her education. Today Naserian dreams of becoming a doctor and building a hospital to help others. She's speaking out, telling girls they have a right to education and that no one can force them into marriage. Dining for Women helped Naserian become a voice of the future in Kenya.

In South Carolina, when Brooke Hammond was sixteen, social media sparked her awareness of the culture of rape and sex trafficking. On Twitter, she read stories like Naserian's and realized how privileged she was, that what happened to Naserian could have happened to her. From her high school economics textbook in a section on women's empowerment, she learned why investing in girls is smart. She started a Dining for Women chapter and plans to expand to other schools, then take DFW with her to college. When I told Brooke she was leading the way like Naserian, she said, "I'm just trying to do what I can. Kids my age are noticing problems in our society that need to be fixed." DFW lets them do that.

SHOWING UP

Looking back on pivotal experiences in my life, I vividly recall being eight, unfolding the message left on my desk, and reading the instructions to meet Diane Green on the playground after school to fight. The act of showing up and witnessing fear evolve into friendship, embedded within me an instinctual understanding of resolving division. At eight, blind courage led me to show up. I never even told my parents. Sometimes you just need to be fearless to learn what you don't know. And should know.

My hope is that we all show up every day and keep showing up until every person gets to wake up with the same opportunities to determine their life stories. In this way my father's legacy lives on eternally.

This book is a gift to you from Norm. An opportunity to see what worked in his life and in mine, and to try something new. Ask yourself his questions. Are you who you want to be? If not, don't wait too long or life might be over while you're still deciding how to live. As Norm would say, "Don't just stand there—do something," and then he'd tell you that "rules are made to be broken."

ACKNOWLEDGMENTS

My husband doesn't believe me when I say I listen to him. Maybe he will when I acknowledge he was the reason I finished this book. It was you, Greg, who walked delicately through minefields when I asked you to read chapters and share your opinions. Thanks for knowing exactly what to say in my ups and downs of self-doubt as a first-time author, and in my grief when I lost both my father, then my mom. Your bravery kept me believing I could do it.

Stepping in at the moment I discovered 470 lifetime writings, I would never have synthesized the enormity of Norm's story had it not been for Nancy Marriott's brilliant editorial coaching that went far beyond what was in our contract. As a Dining for Women member, Nancy understood that his legacy lives on in our mission, and that the world would want to hear Norm's miracle message. My gratitude extends to all who have helped me share his message through this book. When Nancy's work ended, Laura Blume walked into my life and onto every page in the beautiful design of this book as she championed it through the publishing phase.

My gratitude extends to my Dining for Women family whose leadership was so strong, letting me focus on this love story to my father, while they nurtured an ever-strengthening organization. And to my family, who waited patiently to hear what their father, grandfather, great-grandfather wanted to tell them.

ABOUT THE AUTHOR

Barbara Fintel Collins is co-founder of Dining for Women, the largest global giving circle movement dedicated to advancing gender equality and well-being for women and girls around the world. With 470 chapters (and growing) throughout the United States, DFW has educated more than 32,000 global citizens. Together, small gifts have amassed into $7 million in grants to organizations in 60 countries. These grants have directly impacted the lives of 250,000 women and girls, and have created a powerful ripple effect into the lives of one million people in their families and communities.

She believes in creating transformational social change by engaging in DFW's simple model that nurtures community, democratizes philanthropy, and multiplies the power of an individual. Under her leadership, Dining for Women has initiated partnerships with the Peace Corps, UNICEF, OXFAM, and Michelle Obama's Let Girls Learn Initiative. In 2014, Barb was named an Everyday Freedom Hero by the National Underground Railroad Freedom Center.

A graduate of the University of Minnesota with a degree in gerontology, Barb has devoted her career to the nonprofit sector. She and her husband Greg have two grown daughters, and live in Greenville, South Carolina with their gentle husky and feisty cat. Contact Barb by emailing barb@barbarafintelcollins.com or visiting barbarafintelcollins.com.

Made in the USA
Columbia, SC
03 September 2019